TRAILS *and* TRIBULATIONS

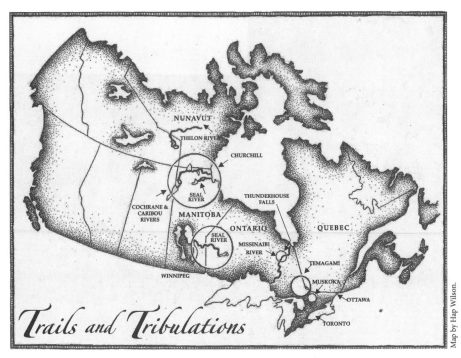

Trails and Tribulations

NUNAVUT

THELON RIVER

CHURCHILL

THUNDERHOUSE FALLS

SEAL RIVER

COCHRANE & CARIBOU RIVERS

MANITOBA

ONTARIO

QUEBEC

SEAL RIVER

MISSINAIBI RIVER

TEMAGAMI

MUSKOKA

WINNIPEG

OTTAWA

TORONTO

On the water trail, time is measured not by the hands of a clock, but by distance accomplished without thinking about it.

TRAILS *and* TRIBULATIONS
CONFESSIONS OF A WILDERNESS PATHFINDER

HAP WILSON

Illustrated by Hap Wilson *and* Ingrid Zschogner

Kingfisher by Ingrid Zschogner.

NATURAL HERITAGE BOOKS
A MEMBER OF THE DUNDURN GROUP
TORONTO

Copy-edited by Allison Hirst
Designed by Courtney Horner
Printed and bound in Canada by Marquis

Library and Archives Canada Cataloguing in Publication

Wilson, Hap, 1951-
    Trails and tribulations : confessions of a wilderness pathfinder / by Hap Wilson ; illustrated by Hap Wilson and Ingrid Zschogner.

ISBN 978-1-55488-397-4

    1. Wilson, Hap, 1951-. 2. Outdoor life--Canadian Shield.
3. Environmentalists--Canada--Biography. 4. Travelers--Canadian Shield--Biography. 5. Park rangers--Canada--Biography. 6. Outfitters (Outdoor recreation)--Canada--Biography. 7. Canadian Shield--Description and travel. I. Zschogner, Ingrid II. Title. III. Title: Confessions of a wilderness pathfinder.

GV191.52.W54 A3 2009   796.5092   C2009-900293-0

1   2   3   4   5   13   12   11   10   09

We acknowledge the support of **The Canada Council for the Arts** and the **Ontario Arts Council** for our publishing program. We also acknowledge the financial support of the **Government of Canada** through the **Book Publishing Industry Development Program** and **The Association for the Export of Canadian Books**, and the **Government of Ontario** through the **Ontario Book Publishers Tax Credit** program, and the **Ontario Media Development Corporation**.

www.dundurn.com
Published by Natural Heritage Books
A Member of The Dundurn Group

Dundurn Press	Gazelle Book Services Limited	Dundurn Press
3 Church Street, Suite 500	White Cross Mills	2250 Military Road
Toronto, Ontario, Canada	High Town, Lancaster, England	Tonawanda, NY
M5E 1M2	LA1 4XS	U.S.A. 14150

To Alexa and Christopher Wilson — two gentle spirits who light my way through the shadows; and to Ingrid, whose energy is matched only by her talent and beauty

TABLE *of* CONTENTS

Indian Archer and Moose by Hap Wilson.

HAP WILSON

Portager into Sunlight by Hap Wilson.

To know that one's trail possessions are packed easily in two loads over the shoulders lightens the burden of care and the want of excess.

INTRODUCTION

One smooth path led into the meadow, and here the little folk congregated; one swept across the pond, where skaters were darting about like water-bugs; and the third, from the very top of the hill, ended abruptly at a rail fence on the high bank above the road ...

— Louisa May Alcott, *Jack and Jill,* 1880

As a kid growing up in rural southern Ontario, I was privy to the numerous trails surrounding the Summit View Golf and Country Club, about forty-eight kilometres north of Toronto. The trails date back to the 1920s, and when my parents bought our house — a heavily treed lot across from the golf course — one of the old ski trails passed through our property. SILVER BIRCH TRAIL was stamped on a diamond-shaped piece of tin, nailed, of course, to a silver birch tree. The tree had grown considerably since the sign was nailed up and was pushing the tin outwards, like butterfly wings, and the printed name was barely discernable. The trail led away from the driveway, not far from the front door of the house, and up a flight of stone steps built to adjust to the steep slope of land that had been bulldozed away some years past.

Up until I had moved there from the outskirts of Toronto, my life had been confined to paved suburban streets, sidewalks, and the school tarmac. And there was the monthly walk to the Willow Theatre on

Saturdays where we would watch double-feature Buck Rogers films for fifty cents, stopping along the way to explore the numerous housing developments evolving out of what vacant land was left. Luckily, we had our grandmother's cottage to escape to in the summertime. Here there were trees, at least, beneath which there were acorns scattered on the ground to collect, low-branched maples to climb and build forts in, and pine trees that proffered fallen dead sticks to brandish as swords and provide kindling wood for the cottage stove.

Across from the cottage road was the dark forest; impenetrable, menacing, glowering, yet strangely beautiful and beckoning. There were no trails to follow so we kids didn't go there. When my father started producing survival films for the Department of Lands and Forests in the late 1950s, he had hired a Native woodsman from the Curve Lake Reserve to work on the film with him. His name was Charlie, and everything he did was magic. He was the first real "Indian" I had met, and he was not at all like the ones on television. When he wasn't working with my father on the sets, Charlie would spend time with my brother and me, showing us how to paddle a canoe, light a campfire, boil water in a birchbark bowl, and most importantly, how to blaze a trail where there was none. He told us that most people *look* but don't *see* and that's how they get lost in the woods. Being lost terrified me.

Charlie took us across the cottage road and into the woods to look for a stand of birch trees some distance away. He went about marking trees with a small axe. "A blaze," he would say in quiet commentary "on both sides of the tree so you can find your way back, *wassakwaigaso mitig.*" He blazed the trees with a deft swipe of the axe, one downward cut, then a right-angled chop to sever the wood chip, revealing the white meat underneath. Sometimes the trees would bleed sap, which was a good thing Charlie had said, because it protected the tree from infection, like a scab over a cut. He blazed the trees at fifty-foot intervals, and when there were no trees, just saplings, he broke one and bent it in the direction he was going (or returning), leaving it pointing like an arrow. Charlie said we'd never get lost as long as we kept our eyes open and remembered what we'd seen, and turned around every so often to see what it would look like on our way back out. "Look at the clouds!" Charlie exclaimed.

"Feel the wind," he would say with a sweeping motion of his big hand. "They'll talk to you and show you the path."

Look. See. Pay attention to detail —the *art* of seeing. The outdoors was like a classroom; you didn't get your knuckles rapped with the pointer when you weren't paying attention, but the natural world did hold you accountable for your actions. I was only six years old then but the time spent with old Charlie, the Anishnabe woodsman, triggered something in my own head that stuck — a bit of old magic that helped me peer into a whole different world.

The best thing about moving north out of the city and into the country was the collection of trails near our house, like the Silver Birch Trail, and it didn't take long for me to explore every one within the first week. I learned that there were absolutely no boundaries, that there would always be a trail somewhere that would lead to someplace I hadn't been before. And when there was no visible trail, I would remember what old Charlie had told me — that the path always appears ahead of you as soon as you put one foot in front of the other.

This anthology of stories is about the wilderness trail, both in the physical sense and, perhaps, as a metaphor for a different path of life that leads us away from the familiar. A trail always leads somewhere, regardless of whether it was human or animal in design. A beaver path up a slope, which I have often mistaken for a portage trail, usually ends abruptly no more than fifty metres from the shore. To the beaver, the trail terminates at a copse of prized birch trees, and the clear path back to the water means a quick retreat from predators — a wolf, perhaps. For me, carrying a heavy canoe and pack over my shoulders, it was a mild annoyance, but it served its singular purpose well for the beaver.

Deer paths through the forest often take advantage of gutways, bench-cut ledges, and areas of light undercover; basically, following the path of least resistance. I have often built trails along deer runs for this very reason; however, unlike the deer, skiers and hikers do not require a clear, straight trail for the purpose of escaping predators.

In the low-lying wetlands, moose will leave a visible trail between ponds and lakes, evidenced by hoof-trough, browse-cuts on willow and alder shrubs, and bark-rubs from antler and teeth marks. These trails are often used as portages and have never required the hand of man to keep clear, save for the occasional removal of a deadfall tree brought down by wind, age, or snow load.

Within the treeline areas of the Far North, caribou leave trails with little apparent care for linear predisposition. Pathways often braid in and out of spruce groves but eventually do arrive at a common river-crossing point or funnel onto a sandy esker — the latter being a sand ridge left by retreating glaciers that now serves as an elevated trailway for both caribou and their predators, the tundra wolf and man. The Sayisi Dene of northern Manitoba and Saskatchewan, unlike the woodland Nations to the south and east who travelled by canoe, followed the sinewy eskers on foot and crossed rivers at strategic locations, usually in pursuit of the caribou. They would bury their dead atop esker trails because it was the only place the summer sun would thaw the permafrost deep enough to enable them to excavate a hole. Thus the trail defined the life essence of the Dene in finite terms — their struggle for survival oftentimes amorphous, dependent wholly on the harmony and reliability of the trail.

The Ojibwa, or Anishnabek, of the eastern woodlands used an interconnecting webwork of summer and winter trails called the *nastawgan*. These ancient trails still unite heart and soul with the spirit of the landscape. And it is with this landscape that most people are vaguely familiar and where a great majority of adventure-seekers find recreation and solace. And yet there are those who continue to defy the natural order of things. Nature — the wilderness — in all its resplendent beauty and magnetism remains intractable. Entering its realm with an imperious attitude shrouds our ability to enjoy fully the benefits celebrated in an untouched world. Living harmoniously is unachievable and life becomes an act of mere survival … and survival is for angry people.

Survival is the art of staying alive. Whether we are in our familiar environment or attempting to find connection with Nature, survival knowledge is essential but not necessarily the mantra that leads us to nirvana. Survival skills comprise but a small percentage of what is actually needed to *live* comfortably in the wilderness. It all depends on what trail you want to follow; the path is not always a clear one.

There are many ways to die in the wilderness. In an age where "survival" shows dominate the airwaves, we tend to fixate on our relationship with Nature in a purely combative way. The true meaning of the "art of survival" and ultimately our aspirations of "living" comfortably within the confines of Nature, of wilderness, are muddled by our perceptions as defined by television and its hedonistic personalities. Not that I have all the answers. I do, nonetheless, have stories to share that may help to affirm that Nature can be neither beaten nor tamed — that our place in the wilderness is simply a logical adjustment to a simpler lifestyle. The correlation between the wilderness trail and our actions eventually becomes our destiny.

The simple reward of the day is a beautiful sunset and sheer exhaustion.

PART ONE
A TRAIL LESS TRAVELLED

The trail through the forest was rough and long unused. In spots the mosses and ground vines had so overgrown it that only the broad scars on the tree trunks, where the lumberman's axe had blazed them for a sign, served to distinguish it from a score of radiating vistas.

— Charles G.D. Roberts from "The Heart of the Ancient Wood," 1900

When you make a pact with yourself that you will never take a job that doesn't entail some sort of wilderness travel, it narrows your options down considerably. It also compromises your ability to make decent money — if that's what's important to you. For me it was the quest for adventure, the open trail, and no boundaries. Money would eventually trickle in somewhere along the way. Survival had a dual meaning — surviving in the bush and surviving in the mainstream. Unfortunately, my wilderness skills evolved quicker than my ability to adjust to civil living.

It's one thing to seek out adventure for personal recreation and satisfaction, but when you make a vocation of it, the dynamics change considerably. Suddenly there are clients to look after, and responsibilities and expectations, and it's no longer a vacation. Well, it is and it isn't;

you try to make it as enjoyable as possible, sometimes against incredible odds. The one thing I've learned along the trail is that you will encounter the unusual, the unexpected, and the untalented. Through all of this, I remain a student of Nature, and recoil at the assertion that I may be anything better than this, or an expert in any field. I am a dedicated survivalist; however, I prefer not to be called that. My ultimate goal for myself, for my family, and inevitably for those who choose to travel in the wilderness with me, is to submit to the pleasures of backwoods travel instead of fighting the elements that define it.

There have been good adventures, and there have been adventures I'd sooner forget. Things happen that you don't expect while wandering through paradise, and they have to be dealt with accordingly. The unwritten laws have not changed for the modern adventurer. *Trails and Tribulations* explores the more obtuse adventure, the senselessness of wilderness politics, and the sometimes psychotic behaviour of the self-seeker.

ONE
CONFESSIONS OF A PARK RANGER

Every great advance in natural knowledge has involved the absolute rejection of authority.
— Thomas H. Huxley (1825–1895)

Before living the quixotic life of a park ranger, I was living the quixotic life but without the steady government paycheque. From the time I finished high school, to the time I was put on payroll as a park technician, I spent six summers, from break-up to freeze-up, in the canoe, doing what any normal, intransigent youth would be doing, I supposed, and it had nothing to do with what was expected of me.

In my renovated chicken-shed-cum-studio, perched on the brim of a hill in the tiny hamlet of Laskay, Ontario, I did my artwork. My mentor Jack McBride, a retired printer, had taken me under his wing and gifted me with the use of his country property, located well outside the dirty fringe of Toronto. There was an adjoining cottage but I preferred the chicken shed as it was easier to heat in the winter. In return for this rather splendid asylum, I supplied him with illustrations for various printing jobs. Also retired were various archaic printing presses that found a home in his basement; together we had quite a business percolating, making assorted greeting cards, hasty notes, posters, and bar mitzvah invitations.

Hap Solo in Canoe by Hap Wilson.

There are no traffic jams on the way to work.

The winter snows piled up against the tiny, un-insulated shack as I scribbled out design after design, persevering, thinking of nothing but the coming spring, saving just enough to grubstake six months of canoeing. In May, when the ice was out, I would be gone.

Forty dollars was enough money to buy supplies each month, as long as I baked (actually fried) my own trail bread — bannock, or what the Anishnabek called *buck-way-ja-gin*. I would also have to fish every other day, eat fresh-water clams (I never liked the rubbery, gritty taste) and pick berries — a veritable feast. Trail fare was simple, life was straightforward and uncomplicated but nothing was prosaic or even predictable. In my early twenties I felt that I could do anything, except, and undeniably so, settle into a conventional lifestyle. After all, I had built cabins and spent the winter in the bush with a school friend, had near-death experiences, been shot at (shot back), been chased by grizzlies and Wyoming buffalo, mauled by wild dogs, climbed a mountain in my bare feet, lost the end of my toe to frostbite, survived a pub-night in Lourdes du Blanc Sablon, been a house-guard for singer Anne Murray, and worked only when I needed money. How could my life become any more idealistic?

But every so often in life as we amble down whatever path we choose to follow, there appears a door, slightly ajar, a shaft of light radiating from the aperture, mystery beyond, opportunity but not without circumstance. I could never resist. It was like discovering a new trail wending its way to somewhere and I needed to know where it would take me … *the quest.* In 1976 I banged on the local government forestry door in Temagami, Ontario. No longer the Department of Lands and Forests but conspicuously more officious, it was now the Ministry of Natural Resources office, buzzing with salaried timber cruisers, district foresters, game wardens, and lands and parks administrators. A woman at the front desk directed me to the lands supervisor, Reg Sinclair.

"You want to do what?" Sinclair smiled inquisitively. I was fully prepared to be rejected, or ejected from his office. "I want to produce a canoe guidebook for Temagami," I explained somewhat timidly, expecting a quick dismissal. Sinclair spun around in his chair and looked out the window at Lake Temagami, taking an inordinately long time to proffer an answer. "And you would chart out all the canoe routes, portages, and campsites?" he questioned. I showed him what I wanted to do on a regional map — to compile all linear recreation trails and canoe routes in a book format that could be used for in-house management and service front-desk inquiries about canoeing in Temagami. But that wasn't the real reason for being there; logging companies had begun accelerated clear-cut operations and were encroaching on my beloved wilderness. Temagami was known for its pine stands, a much valued timber resource. I had this grandiose idea that if I were to document all the threatened canoe routes and publish a guidebook, that backcountry adventure-seekers would flock to Temagami, thereby thwarting the wave of extraction-based industry intrusions. The environmental movement in Canada was picking up momentum, slowly, but some of the developments in northern Ontario gave lobby groups an added punch. The Ontario government, in its myopic wisdom, had slated Temagami's Maple Mountain as a world-class ski resort development, seemingly oblivious to the fact that the mountain (one of Ontario's loftiest peaks) was still revered by the Anishnabek of Bear Island Reserve as a sacred vision-quest and ancient burial site.

"It would make things easier in the office here," Sinclair pondered. "Just sell people the book and that's it — they'll leave happy...." My foot was in the door. Sinclair was an opportunist and he wanted to look good; he knew my idea was a good one.

"When can you start?"

"Tomorrow." I beamed.

I never asked how much money I would be making. Having a steady paycheque every two weeks was a novelty in itself, and I felt somewhat guilty about being paid for canoeing. The office regulars scoffed at what I was doing, but at the time there was money in the parks budget to be spent, and Sinclair had convinced the district manager that my proposal would benefit the province. My explorations, however, dipped outside the district and into three adjoining administrations, and none of these administrators were in the least bit interested in supporting Sinclair in the project. The excuse being that if they made any canoe routes known to the public, they would then be obliged to maintain the routes; and there was also the threat of conflicts between paddlers and logging companies to contend with.

Trails without boundaries; these were ancient travelways for the original people who cared nothing for political barriers on a map. Sinclair's district was the heart of wilderness Temagami — all trails circled back to his administration. I had already paddled the majority of routes in and outside his domain. Anyway, it didn't make sense to research water trails eviscerated by arbitrary precincts. I could accomplish all this in one year — *one year*. That was insane. I would have to paddle a total distance of over 3,500 kilometres in the next six months.

For some inane reason I turned a good paddling friend into a relative and married the girl next door. We would be working together, getting paid handsomely (two paycheques) for doing something we loved (canoeing), and experiencing pangs of guilt as a result. But the guilt didn't last long. Ice-clogged lakes, gruelling portages, incessant biting insects, wind, rain, isolation, and deprivation managed to assuage any feeling of self-reproach. And we accomplished what we set out to do; the book was published, and even with its inherent sloppy first-run production, the book sold out to a demanding crowd of adventure-seekers in short order.

Sinclair was now in a dilemma. The district owned all this research information about Aboriginal canoe routes and portages, and none of it had been maintained, possibly for decades. There was no sense in advertising all these canoe routes if people couldn't have clear portages and clean campsites. The district recreation trails were in a sorry state. There had been a sporadic canoe route maintenance crew sent out in the past but little, if any, work was accomplished. It was a standing joke in the district office — if you were appointed to the job of summer canoe route foreman, it was a summer of heavy drinking at the nearest campsite. Trusting that I could pull this off and make Sinclair's gamble pay off, I was offered a job as chief interior ranger with a mandate to clean up Temagami's backcountry.

There are particular recondite outdoor skills one learns, sometimes by luck and oftentimes out of necessity. When I first started canoeing, mostly through Algonquin Park's most remote regions, there were quite often no distinguishable portage trails present. It didn't mean there were no trails at some time in recent history, it just meant that they weren't obvious anymore. I was forced to look for less conspicuous signs of a trail, or anything other than a barefaced man-painted YOU ARE HERE sign, like those found in tended parks close to the highway.

Next to basic survival, the art of pathfinding was one of Canada's first required occupational skills. Early explorers needed to know where they were going, and they entrusted this job to the most seasoned veterans of the trail, or to Natives who knew the way by familiarity. Since most traffic was restricted to linear canoe routes, almost all trails were dedicated to finding the easiest way around rapids or waterfalls. And sometimes these trails were not always apparent, or the route itself navigable for any great distance. Aboriginal people travelled lightly and left little trace of their passing, but did have an intricate collection of trails. The Ojibwa Nation had an elaborate webwork of summer and winter trails called the nastawgan, some dating back more than five thousand years. The only casual indications left to mark the trails were rock cairns (piled stones) or dolmen markers (large rocks supported by smaller rocks). Over the years the cairns get knocked over and scattered about by bears looking for ants and grubs, and dolmen stones don't always reveal a trail.

I had spent almost ten years already, searching for trails along lake and river routes, getting used to distinguishing animal paths from those tracked by humans. It was a particular challenge to find the best route between lakes that were often kilometres apart; there was the euphoria of discovering a trail that perhaps was used for thousands of years. Many of the trails had been kept open by Ontario's fire brigades — men hired in the early part of the last century to protect the forests from the ravages of wildfires. They travelled by canoe to the remote sections of the wilderness, manning observation towers constructed on hills like Maple Mountain, keeping portage trails clear to enable quick and deliberate movement of supplies and firefighting equipment when called to action. That was long ago, and their movements through the pinelands had been erased by time — axe-blazes grown over, portage markers rotted away, and the linear trough that guided footfall for years now covered deep with leaves, needles, and forest detritus.

Pathfinding, as the skill may have been attributed to early explorations, is all but a lost art. The GPS (Global Positioning System) has replaced our need to depend on basic, once inherent navigational abilities. Even the term *pathfinding* now refers to solving mazes and algorithms, tracing a trail through computer games, or exploring last resort techniques to reduce thermal noise of mirrors and suspensions in gravitational wave, cryogenic ferometric detectors. It has nothing to do with finding your way through the woods.

Temagami presented itself as the ideal place to hone this skill. There were over thirteen-hundred nastawgan trails to be found and, during the year of research for the book, I had managed to locate the majority of trails along all major linear routes, but not without some level of difficulty and frustration. Some trails had already been obliterated by clear-cut logging operations, while other portage routes had been altered by beaver activity; namely, having constructed dams that diverted water flow in a creek, or flooded the pathway so that a new trail had to be blazed. Wildfires had also played havoc while inventorying trails, leaving large areas of scalded, bare rock and blackened stumps, sometimes completely burning off all traces of organic soil. There were also blowdowns from "push-storms" or "micro-bursts" — powerful tornado-like gales that ripped through the district each summer, piling up twisted, fallen trees over the portage trails like giant scattered pickup sticks.

Trails skirting rapids or falls along the river routes were easier to locate than portage trails connecting lake systems. Springtime offered the best inspection of the forest landscape, before the foliage obscured the view; into June when the bush was thick with growth, I would have to get down on hands and knees to scrutinize possible trail configurations — the view a rabbit may have of the understory of leaves and a clear line of sight into the beyond. Oftentimes I would scrape away the top cover of leaf debris to find the cupped hollow of an old footpath that would otherwise be secreted away. Axe blazes on trees had grown over to mere slits; but there was always a signature of some kind, often incomprehensible at first glance, but humbly noticeable through close circumspection.

There were almost a hundred kilometres of portage trails to clear, including the traditional fire tower lookout trails on Maple Mountain and Ishpatina Ridge. For the first two seasons, the MNR district supervisors would not issue us a chainsaw to cut through the long-accumulated deadfall along the trails. It was all axe work — a sometimes dangerous undertaking, especially in blowdowns where fallen trees were suspended and under extreme tension. Communication with head office in Temagami was spotty, at best, since we were out of range with the two-way radio most of the time, and because of this the managers didn't want us cutting off our legs with a saw somewhere back in the bush.

The work was demanding and camp was moved to a new location daily. Slowly, deliberately, and although challenging and arduous, the task of clearing trails was accomplished with unpredicted success. But something was missing. The expected honour and prestige of being an interior ranger did not come with all the anticipated esteem. Life on the trail did live up to the romantic imagery, but within the confines of the district forestry office the deference went to those cutting down the forests, not to those in favour of protecting it.

> *"If a man walks in the woods for love of them half each day, he is in danger of being regarded as a loafer. But if he spends his days as a speculator, shearing off those woods and making the earth bald before her time, he is deemed an industrious and enterprising citizen."*
>
> — Henry David Thoreau

There was no honour in working for the government forestry office. They were fucking everything up. Neil Ayers, a soon-to-be-retired bush pilot working for the MNR, explained it to me emphatically: "... there's been a complete inversion of the bureaucratic triangle. The Ontario Forestry Branch of the thirties, and then the Department of Lands and Forests, operated with only a couple [of] men in the district office filing reports — the rest were out in the field working alongside logging companies, tourist operators, anglers and hunters ... they were in touch with what was going on in the bush."

Ayers was refuelling the Turbo Beaver aircraft, talking as he did routine tasks between flights. I asked him what the difference was today and there was an obvious, intentional edge to his voice: "We're no longer the experts ... there's almost nobody in the field anymore ... we're out of touch. The office is full of forestry technicians plugged in to computers."

So that was it. The forestry office was nothing more than a licensing depot for logging companies and nimrods. Their disorganized and detached management of publicly owned resources and incoherent decisions had catastrophic consequences.

In 1977, a seemingly benign May wildfire got out of hand because the fire crew "pushed" the fire in order to collect overtime pay. Winds came up suddenly and tempered the fire into a raging maelstrom, burning over thirty-five thousand hectares of pine lands. In 1980, a toxic defoliant was accidentally dropped from a helicopter somewhere between Temagami and Cobalt; it was an office joke until trappers began reporting an unprecedented high death rate amongst the beaver population for no apparent reason. The two Junior Ranger camps were being run like detention centres or forced-labour gulags; seventeen-year-old boys were expected to perform all the distasteful duties that the regular full-time employees avoided. Unit foresters, whose job was to supply logging companies with marketable timber, were on the take, according to local mill field supervisor Doug Buck, who ended up working with the new environmental group, the Temagami Wilderness Society, as their personal licensed forester. The minister of natural resources instituted an "open gate" policy on all timber roads in order to beef up the sale of out-of-province hunting licences. But the most disastrous gaffe undertaken by the office was to install radio equipment in the fire tower on Maple Mountain, even after I had told them that it was a gross mistake to do so because of potential vandalism by hikers. It was also a sacred site with potent spiritual energy.

An MNR crew from Sudbury and another from our office were air-dropped on the summit. After they had installed the equipment and were waiting for pickup later that day the weather suddenly turned. Though fog had set in, the helicopter pilot insisted on getting the crews back to their respective bases before dark. Our crew went first but not without difficulty. Because of the high humidity, the windows inside the cockpit steamed over, so that the pilot had trouble orienting the aircraft during liftoff, nearly tipping the rotor blades into nearby trees. After depositing our team back in Temagami, the chopper took off once again for the mountain. He never returned and the fate of he and the four-man Sudbury crew remained a mystery for the next two days.

By the second day after the crash, bears had come to pull the ripe bodies out of the wreckage and started to feast on the corpses. The emergency locating beacon, found on all aircraft, failed to go off after the crash. The cloud and fog was too dense for Search and Rescue to even look for the downed helicopter, but once the skies cleared, it was easy to spot the crash only half a kilometre from the summit. An armed game warden was slung down by chopper to disperse the ravaging bears. Within the month, someone had tossed the radio equipment out of the tower onto the bedrock below.

After eight years I had had enough. My trail and campsite budget had been reduced to a mere pittance, even though the backcountry traffic had increased tenfold over the past few years. Government foresters, not to mention their allies in the industry, had become paranoid because of the rising concern for the environment and the push to create larger wilderness parks. I was disillusioned with a system that didn't work, almost ashamed to be a part of it anymore. There was no glamour in the destruction of wilderness, and even in some obtuse way, I was attached to the organism responsible.

I try to remember my days as a ranger as one of the best times of my life, that I was doing something good for the wilderness and for the people who love to travel its waterways. It was one of the hardest jobs imaginable, but in the end we had cleared over a hundred kilometres of wilderness trails and flown out three thousand bags of packed garbage from campsites. Yet, after almost three decades of conflict, the establishment of token parks, and the shutting down of the Temagami District office, the fight still rages on with no apparent logical end in sight. The only absolute truth in all of this is that everyone is just getting older ... the forest continues to disappear and we have not grown any wiser from our mistakes. My job as a park ranger and technician gave me a privileged view of the inside workings of a bureaucracy that failed Canadians. The deliberately skewed orientation toward the wholesaling of resources consolidated my mistrust of the "system" as a perceived company of experts. And I knew exactly where their Achilles heel was located.

Tandem Canoe with Cliff Face by Hap Wilson.

The trail is not such a lonely place if you talk to ghosts.

TWO
CONFESSIONS OF A
WILDERNESS OUTFITTER

An outfitter *is a company or individual who provides equipment and guidance for the pursuit of certain activities. The term is most closely associated with outdoor activities such as rafting, hunting and fishing, and trail riding.*
— Wikipedia Definition

If you worship the outdoors; if you love Nature in all its splendour; if you are a devoted participant in canoeing, kayaking, hiking, or skiing … then my best advice to you is to *not* go into business as an adventure outfitter. *Why?* Because you become bitter, resentful, stale, cynical, jealous … eventually all of these things take over your psyche. Whether or not you admit it to yourself, it will happen. It's one of the undeniable truths about human nature: We lust after other peoples' freedom.

For me, getting into the business of outfitting people for personal adventures happened inadvertently; a kind of recoil occupation after being disenchanted with the government job as ranger. It was like falling in love for all the wrong reasons — a relationship doomed to fail even though the sex was great. Gear … it's all about gear. And gear is like sex to an outfitter and the outdoor participant — you can never have enough of it. It wasn't always like this. There was a time when outdoor enthusiasts (mostly men at the time) preferred to *blend* with the environment: clothing, boots, tents … *gear*, was always khaki or olive-drab or beryl-green, and equipment was purchased at local army-surplus stores for next to nothing. And it was all natural fibres like cotton, wool, or canvas-duck and leather. It was the adventure that counted and the experience of *being out there* — the journey.

When men met each other at a portage landing at the head of a trail, they would exchange salutations, share a pipe or chew of tobacco, talk about the weather or about fishing and how good or bad it had been. Canoes were heavy, usually canvas-covered cedar with the brand names of Chestnut, Old Town, or Peterborough tagged on the front deck. Glances were exchanged at a man's canoe and how he handled it, carried it, repaired it with Ambroid and bandana and tin-can lid, judged the tightness of his gear load, the care of leather tump and *wannigan* (standard wooden box for carrying kitchen gear and breakables), his trail etiquette and backwoods manner. The constancy of gear and trail mannerisms was conventional, expected, and purposefully drab.

Technology has a way of introducing change and trends whether we want it or not; it's those who market new products who control its success and how it affects our ability to "control" or adapt to the environment. *Control* being the operative word. In the outdoor trade we are constantly trying to control Nature by developing new gear. I know carpenters who are really bad at their trade, but they buy the most expensive tools and all the extraneous gadgetry in an attempt to compensate for lack of skill or knowledge. Technology in the outdoor trade has created a new breed of participant who relies on gear to counterbalance their inherent ineptitude in the wilderness. Gear sluts — people whose main interest in the outdoors is looking good, dressing hip, giving the impression that they actually know what they're doing. Canoeists stumbling along portage trails today strut about as if they were walking a fashion show catwalk, and their gear remains scattered everywhere and always in your way. Talk, if any, is a brief exchange about the lack of signage, or garbage pickup by non-existent rangers, or if the government opened more roads they wouldn't have to portage so much to get into the wilderness. *Do I sound cynical?* I've earned it.

I bought thirty Kevlar canoes and all the related equipment, built a small store, and started selling trips into the wilderness. People came. What I wasn't prepared for was the *type* of person who typically conscripts the services of an outfitter. Generally, these people don't get out very often so they need to rent equipment. And because they don't get out, they tend to lack all or any of the required skills to travel in the wilderness, safely or efficiently. So they wing it, often getting by on random luck. And it didn't matter how good a food package you concocted, or quality of tent and expensive canoe you supplied them with, they — the *client* - meticulously thwarted all your good intentions as an outfitter by not cooking any food at all (eating only the pre-cooked goodies), pitching the tent in a hollow so everyone got wet when it rained, and complaining vehemently that I had rented them a canoe with a hole in it.

There was the church group from Buffalo. Nice people. I rented them expensive Kevlar canoes and life jackets and off they went for a week in the wilderness. As my apartment was directly over the store, I could hear any movement in my equipment yard during the night. I awoke sometime past midnight to find the church group quietly unloading their gear on to the lawn and stuffing the life jackets underneath the canoes. When I confronted them (they were surprised to see me, not knowing that I also lived at my shop), they sheepishly explained that they had had a problem earlier that day. To my dismay, I noticed that the ends of the paddles were all burned and the life jackets were scorched and melted. Upon inquiry, the leader explained that they had to fight a fire, for which, on any normal occasion, trashing my expensive equipment would have been forgivable for having done a noble deed for the sanctity of the wilderness, and at great risk of injury to themselves. But, as it turned out, they had actually started the fire themselves. This was a somewhat common occurrence according to the church director, as all young campers were instructed to burn their toilet paper at the site of excrement (and not safely within the firepit as is normal), and that the odd fire mishap was expected to happen. I assured them that this was not the standard procedure in my woods; shitting incorrectly in the wilderness had its repercussions, and camper-related fires were taken rather seriously. When the government water-bomber and fire crews arrived, the canoeists quickly disembarked from the campsite before they could be held responsible. An entire island was destroyed. Not being a devout Christian, I passed on the name of the church group responsible to the local authorities. They never paid for the damages to my equipment, nor as I recall, ever returned to Temagami.

I was fortunate enough to get out on the occasional guided expedition, a break from the tedium of day-to-day outfitting and of watching everyone else head out on their respective adventures. On one such expedition, I was finishing up a trip on Diamond Lake; it was a nice campsite, quiet, in a sheltered bay. We had just finished dinner and were sitting on the sloped bedrock enjoying the evening calm. A group of six people paddled in and took the campsite across the channel from us — a stone's throw away. I recognized them as a group I had outfitted the day before I left on my trip, Mennonites from St. Jacobs near Kitchener, Ontario. Nice people who booked an unguided complete outfitting package from me. We watched as their group set up camp. The canoes remained tethered along the shore, undulating against the rocks, wearing holes in the hulls. Two men brandishing axes approached a rather sizeable dead tree near the canoes and began chopping it down. It fell directly across the gunwales of a canoe, nearly folding it in half.

Now, I could have yelled out and warned them not to do this, reveal my identity as the owner/outfitter of the canoes, but I was more intrigued by the way in which they would explain this when they returned the equipment the next day. I also have a strict, personal policy not to yell out while on the trail. The purity of silence was paramount. When the canoe-crashers returned their rented gear to the outfitting base, they said nothing about the canoe incident even after being questioned whether the equipment met their satisfaction. I explained that I was the one camped across from them when the tree was chopped down over the canoe causing over three-hundred-dollars damage. They were mildly apologetic but refused to pay for damages contending that "they were renting the canoe, not buying it" and that my insurance should cover it. My insurance wouldn't cover it, I explained, so I tacked the damages onto their bill. Their cheque bounced and I never recovered the money.

A group of jocks brought three new Kevlar canoes back almost completely destroyed. They had run all the rapids on the Temagami River in low water. It was also reported by another guiding company that my clients had filled their canoes with packs and skidded the boats over the rocky portages, not once carrying them across the trail. Since I always took a refundable cash deposit for canoes (usually not enough to pay for most accrued damages), I could at least hold back the deposit made. Not only did the jocks refuse to pay for damages, they insisted I give them back their damage deposit.

Tents would come back with knife slices in the floor, sodden with mud and with crushed mosquitoes pasted to the inside walls; pot sets would be caked with burned-on food, black with soot; packs missing straps that had been ripped off their seams; sweaty sleeping bags that needed dry-cleaning, sometimes too grungy to keep at all; broken axes and saws; lost life-jackets and paddles, trashed canoes ... But it was the cavalier way in which all this gear was returned after the trip that really bothered me. Where was the sense of pride and care in the maintenance of equipment that was part of one's essential kit — the survival material that one depends on? People just didn't care anymore; they didn't care because they knew their visit to the wilderness was transient, and that they would return promptly to their contrived and safe boxes in the city, and to their disposable-wracked lifestyles, dishwashers, and twice-a-week garbage collection. Trail lifestyle was hit or miss and lacked the finesse engaged by seasoned wilderness travellers, or those who cared. There were, on occasion, considerate clients who tended their rental outfit as if it was their own, but not enough of them to assuage the aggravation suffered through an almost constant barrage of malperforming neophytes seeking packaged adventure.

The Client would complain about almost everything, and it was usually about things in Nature that we have absolutely no control over — the weather, biting insects, the wind always in the wrong direction, the difficulty of portage trails and *where was all the wildlife?* As if they expected moose and bear and wolves to be lined up along the shores waiting for their pictures to be taken.

"When did you break camp?" I'd ask them.

"You mean pack up and leave in the morning?"

"Yes, what time?"

"Ten o'clock or so, maybe later."

As it turned out, most paddlers and other outdoor folk know little or nothing about wildlife habits or about the environment in which they live. Our modern expectations of the Wild — its nuances, patterns, complexities, peculiarities, and appearance, is governed by what the media feeds us — *the Disney fixation* — wildlife performing in unnatural ways. Actual or anthropomorphized animations of creatures fail to differentiate what's real and what's fantasy, and confound our ability to raise our consciousness about the outdoors.

Canoeists who sleep through the morning, the time when many species of wildlife are most active, miss out on a possible experience. Paddlers who bang their paddles on the gunwales of their canoes, or are inordinately noisy, also fail to "get the picture." Campers who leave garbage or human excrement around their campsites, on the other hand, are sure to have a wildlife encounter sooner or later.

But not all outfitters are derisive about the business as I am. Some could overlook the slack-mindedness, almost innocent naivety of the modern adventurer and turn it into something positive. I tried. Times were changing. The backwoods trail attracted a new genre of explorer, bred from a narcissistic society and an ever-changing definition of *wilderness*. The good thing that came out of my occupation as a canoe trip outfitter was the number of people I would pump into the backwoods, and at a time when we needed to show strength in our own industry. And, in a way, that worked to the advantage of the environmental movement, at least to illustrate to the government that there was more to the woods than just stump value and hunting licences.

THREE
CONFESSIONS OF A WILDERNESS GUIDE

It's the way you ride the trail that counts.
— Dale Evans

Although I had been guiding wilderness trips for several years as a park ranger, my first commercially guided expedition under my own company name wasn't until 1984. My bush skills were adequate but my ability to knit people together in a group trip dynamic was deficient. I was eager to lift my new outfitting company off the ground and I took bookings for guided trips with insufficient client scrutiny. I was elated that I could book ten guys on a river trip in May, just after ice-out; any bookings in the pre-season was a commercial boon. Cash flow was paramount.

Bill was the client group-leader and he assured me that everyone who signed up had the required whitewater canoeing skills. The Makobe River in spring flood was a tempestuous little river and there was little room for error. John Kilbridge, canoe builder and former trail ranger, would be my assistant. Within the mélange of clients was a heart surgeon, company CEO's, and one blind man. Terry was a musician, legally blind but could make out some vague outlines of rocks and trees. We were air-dropped to Banks Lake at the headwater of the river for a four-day flush downriver in ice-cold water with little time for instruction.

Hap Standing by Ingrid Zschogner.

Let me tell you about stress.

Everyone paired off, the insurance man and the heart surgeon together in one canoe but sitting backwards in their seats, the bowman's feet crammed into the tiny space behind what was supposed to be the stern seat. He complained about the lack of space for his legs until I corrected him as to which end of the canoe was to point forward. As it turned out, none of the ten men had ever run any moving water and only four had any experience at all.

"How hard can it be?" Bill the leader pleaded. John and I looked at each other in quiet consternation. It began to snow. We managed to nurse the first four client-canoes down the initial rapids, an easy class 1, but with one boulder in mid-channel to manoeuvre around. The doctor and the insurance man weren't so lucky. Their canoe broached the only rock in the rapids, tipped upstream, and filled with water. The two men were able to step up onto the boulder but were now twenty-five metres from shore, stranded, cold, and wet. John and I beached our canoe and ran back up the shore. My new Kevlar canoe was wrapped around the boulder. John reminded me that the clients were more important than the state of the canoe — we'd worry about the boat after we got the men safely to shore.

The two men were soaked to the bone, shivering in the cold, but we managed to walk them through the rapids back to shore, rescued their packs and instructed them to change into dry clothes. Extricating the wrapped canoe from the boulder would not be easy. It had to be done quickly as everybody was starting to feel the effects of the cold and we needed to get to our campsite before dark. I waded out to the canoe with a stout spruce pole and began levering the canoe off the boulder while John spotted from shore. Canoe rescue techniques had not yet been developed, such as the Z-drag rope method, and some broached canoes just won't budge under that amount of hydraulic pressure. But I was lucky. The broken canoe slid off the boulder, taking me with it and down the rapids. John jumped into the river and grabbed my arm and helped me to shore and the two of us managed to haul the swamped canoe into shallow water. John took the clients ahead to the campsite downriver while I tried to patch the wrecked canoe as best as I could with duct-tape. By the time I reached camp it was dark but the group was in good spirits.

We were fortunate back then; it could have turned out differently. I made several mistakes, none of which were attributed to particular bush skills. My capacity to analyze the client, to judge their inherent capabilities, needed work — *a lot of work*. It was a harsh wake-up call. I was responsible for all these people, legally liable and potentially at risk from lawsuit if anything happened. I was relying on skill alone … and that was only a modicum of the talent that was required to be a good guide.

Everybody has their own brand of idiosyncratic weaknesses — baggage they carry with them — some more than others. But for the adventure-seeking client, it's likely to spill out while under duress three hundred kilometres from the nearest road. And it happens for various reasons: exhaustion, isolation, fear, inability to cope, biting insects, weather, cold, incessant wind, and even personality conflicts with other clients. Put eight or ten individuals together in a tight social troupe, outside their familiar parameters, and vault them into the wilderness, and you have the making of one of two things; hopefully, what you get is unadulterated adventure but, if things go awry and the guide doesn't have his or her shit together, you can stir up a dangerous mix of anarchy and mutiny, not to mention the potential lawsuits from gross fuck-ups.

Since my first commercial expedition in 1984, I've learned a lot about the human psyche and how it functions, or dysfunctions, under stressful conditions. Guiding skills, the *hard-skills,* like making a fire, setting up camp, negotiating rapids, are only a small part of what is required to be a proficient guide. A qualified guide (beyond the first-aid or other accreditations) needs to be a facilitator, a backwoods bon-vivant chef, an entertainer, and a teacher. But what about the remaining 75 percent of skill requirements? Basic skills are easy to learn, over time, but the most difficult facet of guiding (and the most underrated), is the ability to "read" personality traits. One learns to "read" weather or "read" rapids, but to adequately justify taking a group of neophytes into the wilderness and assaulting them with all manner of environmental conditions, the guide needs to be able to sense what's going on inside everybody's head.

When I book a full compliment for an expedition, say eight individuals, I know that at least two people will have sociopathic tendencies — it's a given statistic and product of our social makeup in an aggressive, self-indulgent, consumer-based world. Two others in this group will have recently suffered through some kind of personal trauma — a death in the family or of a close friend, a break-up with a partner, trouble at work perhaps. An additional two clients will be rife with self-doubt, unable to make spontaneous decisions. The last two people will be well-rounded and competent, reliable and helpful but possibly short on patience because of the other clients' ineptitude. The guide then has to make an assessment of each and all of these personalities *before* the client is even accepted onto the roster of participants. The guide, as booking agent, is often responsible for selecting the group participants, scrutinizing their abilities, and the general compatibility in a group function.

Before establishing a more rigorous screening process, I once booked four hardcore Marines from California and teamed them up, by chance, with four gay men from Toronto. Sexual persuasion is not something you ask about when signing up individuals for a wilderness expedition. Not that I would have turned either the Marines or the gays away from participating. I would have made more effort to match up such disparately different personalities with likeminded people. Composing a workable and companionable group of clients from the get-go ultimately makes the guide's job easier. Unfortunately, some maladjusted and neurotic client may sneak through the selection process and the guide then has to meld this potentially explosive personality into the group. And it has to be done quickly. It's like a foot blister. If it's not dealt with at the onset, it could grow into a debilitating problem; and this will have a deleterious affect on the group.

Ben signed on to one of my two-week whitewater trips, a late arrival and a friend of a friend who met through an internet dating company. He was a lawyer. In all respects he seemed appropriate to fit into this group; he had experience in moving water, correctly answered all the pre-trip questions — there was no reason to deny his participation. I now had a full complement of clients to round out this expedition.

Ben was a Type-A personality — like many of my clients — like the majority of the more ardent adventure-seekers. These people can be described as impatient, excessively time-conscious, highly competitive, and incapable of relaxation; a lot of these people have free-floating hostilities that can be triggered by minor incidents; some may exhibit sociopathic tendencies, or *dissocial personality disorder.* Ben was a classic example. People with DPD generally have callous unconcern for the feelings of others and lack the capacity for empathy, disregard social norms, seldom profit from experience, and are persistently irritable.

There are those ostentatious individuals who insist on challenging the authority of the guide, especially on whitewater river expeditions — those people who think they possess skills over and above the leader. This is evident at the first set of rapids encountered. In most cases, allowing the "show-off" to screw up early on in the trip is enough to humble them back into the group dynamic successfully. With Ben though, having been allowed to run the first rapid unsuccessfully while everyone else watched, was not the self-effacing experience expected. He wanted another run at it. I declined his request. After a week of persistent challenges, running rapids without permission while everyone else portaged, and multiple rescues, I took Ben aside from the group and threatened to leave him behind on the trail — to wait for a floatplane to pick him up. His response was, "Try it."

At a particularly dangerous chutes, on day ten, Ben snuck back to the portage trailhead and, instead of carrying his canoe and pack around the chutes, he ran the falls. A French guide drowned here a year later. Below the chutes we watched in horror as Ben's overturned canoe tumbled over the precipice, followed by a canoe pack and then Ben himself, clutching his paddle. Almost swept into a hydraulic souse hole, a place where it would be impossible to rescue him, he was finally flushed into a recirculating eddy. Trapped, but safe, Ben arced around in wide circles while we watched from shore. The group had had enough of Ben by this time and the collective decision was to sit on the shore and eat lunch while Ben remained stuck in the eddy. We pulled his canoe and pack out of the river but left Ben floating for a good half-hour before rescuing him.

Despondent but compliant, Ben finally understood his boundaries; and after threatening to sue me, my heirs and assigns, calmed down enough to reintegrate (but not completely) back into the group.

The outdoor adventure product trade panders to Type-A personalities, profits from their innate and insatiable appetite for gear, and is somewhat responsible for creating a new genre of adventure jockey — *the Collector.* The Collector hoards gear … expensive gear. And these people often sign up for the more exotic adventures because they have the money to do so. They have little interest in history, or geophysical attributes, spirituality, cultural amenities, or even the general aesthetic makeup of the landscape of a particular adventure destination. They choose a particular adventure for its notoriety. And they will do this trip once only and then move on to another, and another. Some people collect adventure trips like other people collect stamps. There's nothing really creative or deeply enlightening about it.

I terminated the participation of a couple of collectors while guiding a Thelon River expedition. It was on the third day of the trip and due to heavy winds we had to be evacuated to a new location further upriver — a change in the itinerary. Although agreeable to the change, two participants began drinking heavily, became aggressively antisocial to the point I had to have them flown back to Yellowknife without a refund. As wilderness guide, I have the authority to make this decision — to change an itinerary for the safety of the group, and to remove any potential or disruptive influence that may compromise the group well-being. You can pay seventy thousand dollars to climb Mount Everest, but no self-respecting guide will guarantee that you will ever get to the summit. In my case, these two men attempted to sue me for changing the itinerary; they had paid money to paddle the Thelon River, and I took this trophy away from them.

Then there were the twins — two anorexic, neurotic thirty-two-year-olds who signed on to a whitewater clinic along with the "stalker." The stalker was an attractive Jewish lady who was married to a doctor. The two of them wanted to join one of my whitewater clinics but she insisted on bringing her friend along, one-half of the twins. Only the twin wouldn't come without her suicidal sister who was lamenting the loss of her lover by locking herself in her bedroom for a year. And the lover was the best friend of the doctor. The doctor wouldn't come without his mother and another gentleman friend, and in the end, the two twins had decided to bring along a young man who they had just met. They were to drive to Temagami to catch the floatplane and I would meet them at a designated spot along the Lady Evelyn River. The water levels were high and as it was springtime, the black flies were particularly irksome.

In my opinion, Temagami is a rather unprogressive town. It prides itself in its ability not to attract business or tourists. The docks at the air service, though, did well and pandered to sportsmen who often milled about waiting for flights amidst skids of cased beer, coolers, and fishing paraphernalia. It being the opening of walleye fishing season, the air service was seasonally busy. When my group arrived they had a two-hour wait for their plane. To make the time go faster, the twins smoked a couple of joints to relax and had removed most of their clothing and, after a while, began fondling, caressing, and performing carnal gestures on the strut of the Cessna 185 moored at the dock, much to the amusement of the air service staff and patrons. In no time, half the men of the village had descended upon the air service for the free show. Upon the twins' arrival in the Wilderness Park, they had still not dressed adequately to ward off the black flies which by now had zoned in on the promise of new flesh to alight on. As they stepped off the plane I made a mention that they may want to slip something on for protection but received a "fuck-you" look of contempt instead. In the least, I asked if they could put on a pair of shoes, which also was received with equal defiance. What they did next actually took me by surprise. They walked over to a slough of muskeg and began rolling in it, coating themselves liberally in the mud, which, of course, was their answer to the problem of biting flies. *The trip was going well so far,* I mused silently, thinking of how interminably long the week was going to be.

Things got more bizarre. The stalker had insisted that I was her soulmate and that we should be together, and that my wife should be with her husband. The husband by now was taking the brunt of criticisms from his wife, I was trying desperately to deflect the coquetry of the stalker, and the jilted twin who was locked in her bedroom for a year had slipped into a deep funk about life in general and took me to be some sort of power monger. While out gathering firewood, I had returned to the campsite to find a hundred candles lit through the woods during a time when there was a fire-ban caution imposed. Admittedly, I was a bit excited about a potential fire in the dry bush and had the candles extinguished promptly. I was thoroughly brow-beaten for this and paid the price. The one twin wasn't dealing with the trip very well; the bugs, the heat, the work, the need to wear clothes and shoes, my authoritarianism. The stalker came to me and said her friend's sister was going to commit suicide and what was I going to do about it. By this time I had just about had enough of the twins so I unsheathed my knife and handed it to the stalker to give to the twin. Nobody saw the humour in this but me.

Oddly enough, nobody died on this trip, whether by their hand or by mine; but some trips have a residual complexity to them, as did this one. The stalker called my wife up after the whitewater clinic and demanded that she get divorced — free me so the stalker and I could be soulmates. Unlike some other wilderness guides who would take advantage of such situations, I had a strong personal code of ethics not to get involved with clients. This situation, however, did nothing to consolidate that mantra with my wife.

People have different reasons for signing up for wilderness trips. Personal reasons, of course, such as being able to meet new friends they wouldn't naturally meet anywhere else. There are a lot of lonely individuals who use this particular venue to eke out a new relationship, the guide often being the prime objective — married or not. And guides (generally speaking) have this cavalier disrepute of being womanizers. I've met other, younger, and mostly unmarried wilderness guides who imbibe in contests to see who can bed the most clients in a running season. The opportunity is rife with desperate, lonely women.

Late one fall I had a call to organize a long weekend canoe trip for a company that sponsored teenagers in transition. I was a little hesitant to take the group just by scanning through their list of requirements which included taking along a body-bag. Granted they had had mishaps on their trips, usually because of poor guiding and cut-rate costs, but I was used to late season guiding. It wouldn't be difficult.

The counsellor was in her late twenties, a good leader and helpful. That was a good thing because one of the girls on the trip was eight-months pregnant, and teenagers at the best of times were high maintenance. It was an easy route that took advantage of large campsites, big enough to accommodate the twelve of us and four tents. The boys resided in one tent, the girls in the other, while their counsellor and I each had our own tent. After the first night out it became obvious that the counsellor had something else on her mind. I assured her that I was married and didn't get involved with clients. She stormed off, practically ripping her tent from the ground, the bevy of teenagers consoling her (they were in on the whole affair), none of whom talked to me for the rest of the paddle out.

Invitations appeared more often than I like to relate and I never saw myself as the receptor for such activities, but I was astounded as to the level and extent some people would go to have an affair while on the adventure trail, either with the guide or with another client. It can present some uncomfortable situations and the guide — as perceived by definition of the career — is often deemed "available" simply by brandishing that romantic, free-spirited, and attractive lifestyle. My last marriage was founded on such notions that the guide's social science was one of liberality and leisure. And it often is, except that a marriage with an ideal, or the promise of capturing that nomadic temperament and boxing it, is surely destined to fail. It's the trail that is important to the guide, first and foremost; and when the guide comes home he is often temperamental, moody, unsociable, and happy only by planning the next expedition. And the trail beckons, always, as a conduit of freedom.

The wilderness trail either brings out the best in people or the worst. Thankfully, the majority of people I have had as clients made a connection with self, others, and the environment around them. But as forgettable as a string of sunny days, it's the rogue storm one remembers. The guide does not have the privilege to go home after work; he is committed to these people twenty-four hours each day until the trip is over.

But to what extreme and by which drastic measure can a wilderness guide take in keeping a sense of order. A captain of a boat can throw a man in the brig and he's safely alienated from the rest of the passengers. On a wilderness canoe trip, in comparison, the guide doesn't have the convenience of a retention system. I've only once had an incident when a psychotic adventurer needed to be subdued. And he was my paid assistant. It was the only time in my career when it was necessary to use a firearm as a solution to a dangerous situation. This particular episode is covered in detail in "River of Fire" later on in the book.

But in some cases the guide is not always right. There are times when the guide is under pressure from time constraints, pure exhaustion, and even peer pressure. Younger, less seasoned guides are often more likely to make errors in judgment than the veterans. In 1977, while I was employed as park ranger, one of the worst canoeing tragedies unfolded on the Ottawa River, within my own district. A group of fourteen students and two teachers (acting as guides), upset in the middle of the river in June while making a rough water crossing. Twelve students and one teacher died of hypothermia. Instead of waiting for calm weather, or rafting their canoes, the guides made the decision to cross a deadly piece of water just to keep to a tight schedule.

Even experienced guides perish, and this is typically the fate of those who defy their own abilities and common sense. A good guide knows the limit of knowledge and physical capacity that sets personal and group boundaries. Venturing beyond this principle opens up a quagmire of potential tribulations. Climbers often attempt to push their personal limits. Climbing is a completely self-indulgent sport and there are a plethora of famous mountain guides whose bones decorate the fool's abyss. This happens when the level of risk is greater than the guide's capacity to mitigate the unknowns … and in the wilderness there are always going to be uncharted and enigmatic trails.

It is said that fear is the mother of safety, and it is fear that intensifies an adventure trip. It is our basic survival mechanism and is an instinctive reaction caused by rising adrenalin levels. On whitewater river expeditions the adrenalin pulses with the current flow; the sound of rapids ahead prompts the heart to beat faster and the sweat to bead on the forehead. The unknown looms ahead. But there is no adventure if there is no risk, and when we tempt fate and step closer to the edge, there will always be an element of fear. A balanced sum of trepidation makes us wary; too little or too much fear makes us stupid. Fear conditioning is a part of the guide's expected competence as a leader. The guide is expected to be stoic, fearless, intrepid, and responsive to any situation. Anything less could have disastrous effect on the well-being of the group. When anything goes wrong, everyone looks to the guide for a responsible and quick solution carried out with proficiency. And there are times, even for me as a seasoned guide, when fear is overwhelming and you find yourself grasping for a way out that remains elusive and improbable. The once tight ship starts to list to one side and everyone grabs for the handrails. Luckily, there is always a Plan B to put into play to counter all of Murphy's Laws, or should be, in the guide's bag of tricks.

I like being a guide. Unlike the role of an outfitter where life can be prosaic and predictable, venturing beyond the line of civilization with a group of eager patrons has a particular appeal to me. It's not about power, although in the eyes of the client, the guide is often revered as a superhuman empyrean figurehead. Ego aside, the task comes with no shortage of challenges. And it is the capricious nature of the business, the alluring changeable trail of discovery that is attractive. And to see the wilderness through the eyes of those debutants, the children of Nature who view the sacredness of the landscape for the first time, to feel their excitement, to share in the journey in the most primitive way, defines my rationale for loving the guiding life.

FOUR
CONFESSIONS OF A TRAILBUILDER

As a single footpath will not make a path on the earth, so a single thought will not make a pathway in the mind. To make a deep physical path, we walk again and again. To make a deep mental path, we must think over and over the kind of thoughts we wish to dominate our lives.

— Henry David Thoreau

According to statistics, 90 percent of people think trails just *happen.* They appear inexplicably over the carapace of the Earth. It is one of those incontrovertible realities that go unnoticed, unquestioned ... like the fissures in the bark of a giant white pine, the veins on a leaf, they materialize in front of us but we think little about how they got there.

The remaining 10 percent of folk have built a trail, somewhere in their lives, and know something about the disposition and temperament of trail building.

In March of 2007, I attended the Professional Trail Builders Association annual convention. Held in Reno, Nevada (of all places), it was a gathering of eclectic and somewhat eccentric trailbuilders, trail managers, park administrators, and industry representatives flogging the latest in soft-track excavators, gas-powered wheelbarrows and new-

The best part about wilderness trail building is the lifestyle.

fangled hand grubbers. The main casino floor of the hosting hotel was abuzz twenty-four hours a day, non-stop with all the tawdry hoopla that inspires people to throw away their money. Upstairs in the boardroom was a gathering of the clan; bearded, suspender-jeaned trail engineers (old hippies), IMBA (International Mountain Bike Association) bicycle jockeys, and backcountry trail experts. It was an almost comical conjugation of two divergent cultures. In the least, the Reno scene inspired the convention theme, somewhat as a religious experience in the den of iniquity.

I attended the conference as a representative trails specialist for a resort I was working for in Muskoka, Ontario — the first J.W. Marriott luxury hotel in Canada. Three years before, billionaire owner, Ken Fowler, asked if I would construct trails in a one-thousand-acre reserve at the resort.

"You're dangerous." Fowler pointed his finger at me from across a table at our first meeting. He knew that I was an environmental activist with a bit of history.

"Yes, and you have to be accountable," I replied. The elderly developer laughed at my pointed response. He agreed to protect at least half of the land purchased for the resort to be set aside for non-mechanized trail construction. I was to build a world-class trails system because the resort had little else to bank on as far as attractive amenities. They sent me to Reno to scope out the latest in sustainable trail-building techniques. I still had much to learn about constructing a good trail.

When I worked as a park ranger, there were no guidelines for constructing trails. You were handed a chainsaw and told to cut a trail from point A to point B, regardless of what was in between. Although I was cautious and careful enough when I did cut a new trail, there was no concern for the ecology of the landscape, nor any understanding of possible despoliation of the environment in the way of foot-trampling effects, proximity to bird nesting sites, or sensitivity of thin bedrock soils. You axe-blazed a rough pathway, in as straight a line as possible, then slashed your way through with a chainsaw. It was brutal. There was no art to it. That was almost thirty years ago.

Sustainable trail building is now considered an art and a sometimes complex engineering feat. There are more than twenty sciences involved, from understanding soil types, hydrological patterns and sensitive ecological attributes, to social and cultural elements (who walks a trail and why?) to consider. Constructing trails with a straight-line, Point A to Point B mindset adhered to an archaic, linear disposition; trails now take on a life of their own in temperament and configuration — straight lines were shunned, giving way to the evolution of the "stacked loop"... Point A now returns to Point A. It's not so much the destination of the trail that is important, but the journey that unfolds along the way that counts. People prefer to walk in circles rather than on one-way-return trails.

It's the same when designing water trails. Canoeists much prefer travelling in a loop if they're on a lake trail; rivers are different since they run one way only. The more popular canoeing parks and reserves like Algonquin, Quetico/Boundary Waters, and Temagami, all have circular route blueprints. When I started designing water trails for Temagami, and later for the Province of Manitoba, I was relying on my own investigations with the aid of outdated and inaccurate trip records. Between the sixties and the eighties, it was common practice for the district forestry offices to analyze and record portage trails by aerial reconnaissance. Generally, a summer forestry student was hired to plot trails by sheer guesswork and estimation while peering out a window of an aircraft moving at 120 kilometres per hour. Locations of trails were oftentimes assumed to be where they should be (using the linear method of the shortest distance between points). The coarse, irregular topography of the Canadian Shield landscape defines where a trail can be established. Sometimes trails are located some distance from the assumed spot, having been determined by an impassable marsh or precipitous escarpment. People of the First Nations obviously knew the land better than anyone and established trails to adapt to the landscape; for me, it was necessary to think cognitively from the Aboriginal perspective and not through the eyes of a district planner. Establishing a new trail is systematic and uncomplicated — you didn't have to worry about any historical or cultural references. You scouted the physical layout, avoided steep terrain where possible, flagged the trail, and then cut it out. It was a simple process. Locating primitive or historical trails was another matter. If there are no visual orientations then you rely on your power of intuitive understanding — a kind of sixth sense. You get the *feel* for where the trail once was or should be; you walk it over and over again, both ways, somewhat like trying on a new pair of shoes and walking around the store in them — if they fit, then you buy them. If the trail "fits," then you can comfortably clear it out. Once the brush, snags, and footfalls are removed and you carry your gear over the trail, there is a sense of elation born of resurrecting a piece of cultural history (not to discount the ease in which the gear was now carried over the cleared trail).

I've been building trails for almost thirty years. I'm a little obsessive-compulsive about it. I'm constantly surveying the landscape while I drive along the highway, looking at places where trails could be built along lakesides, up to the apex of an escarpment, a farmer's field. I visualize the finished trail and me riding my bicycle along it, or trekking up some bluff with a pack on my back. It's a sickness, I know, I own and wear my neurotic habits on my sleeve. And when I walk, ski, or bike along a trail that I didn't design and build, I scrutinize its construction in minute detail. I'm hopeless.

But trail building is addictive, and I sort out the habitual compulsion to build trails by building more trails. If I'm not building my own trail on my property, somebody else will want a trail constructed somewhere. And trails are more popular today than ever before, for whatever activity so long as it adequately provides an experience for the user; and the more trails we have, the more places there are for people to show off their outdoor gear, get some exercise, and enjoy Nature.

There is something of the sublime in trail building as an art, and like any skill it reflects the personality of the one who created it. This is true of anything built of the hand — a gratification that your labour will be enjoyed by someone else. It is one of the hardest jobs I have ever undertaken; physically, it demands a firm grasp of the realities of the earth-environment. Trails are scribed easily over mineral soil but Canada's predominant landscape of rock can make trail work tenuous. Psychologically, it requires an ability to cope with all of the extraneous natural forces that humankind and science have tried to quell for years — weather, biting and stinging insects. Trails constructed by mechanized means (dozers, skid-steers, and excavators) are not really trails but "troads," hand-built trails are the true footpaths that spare the environment the abuse. The Pulaskis, Italian hoes, grubbers, loppers, rakes, and shovels touch the earth lightly; tree roots are landscaped into the trail instead of being ripped apart; a salamander and its home of mossy log is gently and reverently moved to one side of the working trail; the path meanders between gargantuan pines just wide enough for people to walk between and certainly too narrow for the passing of a Komatsu bulldozer.

Public parks and their planners often design and over-build a trail to the extent that it looks contrived, unnatural and over-tended. Their rationale behind this is to placate to the apparent needs of the physically challenged, and certainly this is something of a consideration. Many of my own clients have had various degrees of physical challenges, but their opinion of super-groomed trails comment that they only help to accentuate their "disability." They want to enjoy Nature the same as anyone else, granted there aren't any precipitous climbs or stairs, they can manoeuvre quite well on their own along a natural pathway.

The administrations in some canoeing parks, like Algonquin in central Ontario, have taken the initiative to turn historic portage trails into veritable roads, mostly through "make-work" programs. Log-lined, wood-chipped "troads" have replaced the traditional trail, severing its conservative charm and purpose. Obtrusive signs are erected directing people where to walk, where to crap, where to put their garbage and where to pitch their tent … and this is in a wilderness park setting. But it's what the general adventure public has come to expect when embarking on an outing — without signs we are lost.

As a ranger in Temagami, at the time there was a collective agreement amongst user-groups that signage would not be posted anywhere in the wilderness. It was conceived that any man-signs would detract from the experience. A simple change in district administration and a planner's suggestion often becomes policy. Signs were eventually placed along ancient trailways so that modern campers could find their way … instead of having to rely on primitive instincts. Temagami district officials still have a tough time keeping their signs posted as the old, traditional paddlers keep taking them down.

One individual who has not enough to do to keep himself occupied in a worthwhile manner, has taken it upon himself to mark every portage with strings of fluorescent orange flagging tape, whether it needs it or not. Trail entrances are ringed with festoons of the tape, hanging like Tibetan prayer flags, half of which the birds retreat with for nest material, or the sun breaks it down into bits of wind-blown garbage. The trail itself is then marked every twenty metres or so with yet more tape. I'm forever removing scads of tape while on my own trips.

At a recent ceremony hosted by my Ojibway friend, Alex Mathias, Mr. Flagging Tape was there and boasting of his travels and trail marking. Of course, we got into a fray about the flagging tape of which he maintained was necessary so that the city canoeists wouldn't lose their way. I turned to Alex and asked how his people ever found their way without the advent of flagging tape. Alex just laughed. "We just knew where to go, we didn't need no signs," he said. "But white man needs all the help he can get."

Tree Spiker by Hap Wilson.

The green terrorist.

FIVE

CONFESSIONS OF AN
ENVIRONMENTAL ACTIVIST

Moderation? It's mediocrity, fear, and confusion in disguise. It's the devil's dilemma. It's neither doing nor not doing. It's the wobbling compromise that makes no one happy. Moderation is for the bland, the apologetic, for the fence-sitters of the world afraid to take a stand. It's for those afraid to laugh or cry, for those afraid to live or die. Moderation ... is lukewarm tea, the devil's own brew.

— Dan Millman, *The Way of the Peaceful Warrior*

There is something deliciously alluring about defying the general order of things. Rebelling against the system is a little like outdoor adventure — it adheres to all the fundamental criteria that combine risk with pleasure and a grab-bag of unknowns. There is an obvious or prescribed goal, the journey in getting there (with an element of risk), and a reward at the end. The reward is not a tangible entity; it's the sheer elation in having participated. Dissention has a further purpose and compensation — there is an uplifting of the spirit — *the fight for a cause.*

Writing this chapter was difficult for me as there were possible implications that I could be involved in subversive actions against logging companies whose method of tree "harvesting" is to clear-cut every living species in a given area. And I say "given" figuratively because government forestry offices are only too generous in gifting companies with huge tracts of timber — the "harvesting" of wood fibre that often does not reflect local jobs. There are, however, some acts of defiance that I can write about with a certain amount of selective detachment.

Ecotage is a portmanteau of the *eco* prefix and *sabotage*. It is used to describe (usually) illegal acts of vandalism and violence, committed in the name of environmental protection. As a term, it goes back to 1972 and predates the more recent neologism, "eco-terrorism." Ecotage is also referred to as "ecodefence" or "monkeywrenching." Nineteen seventy-two was a hallmark year for a lot of things. A band of counterculture hippies from the Don't Make a Wave Committee, from Vancouver, British Columbia, founded a new environmental group called Greenpeace; in Ontario, a troupe of wily canoe-heads assembled to form the Save Maple Mountain Committee, in turn giving confidence to the local Native band to slap a ten-thousand-square-kilometre land claim in the face of the provincial government.

I had been canoeing in Temagami for three years and Maple Mountain was a pivotal icon in the heart of the ancient pinelands. The ensuing fight to protect the mountain from being developed into a world-class ski resort became a national issue. The Native land claim effectively put a block on specific development within the district (mining, prospecting, and cottaging), but it was still business-as-usual for the logging companies who were penetrating the wilderness with intrusive roads. By 1978 — the year I was conscripted by the government to maintain the district portage trails — Maple Mountain became the vital focal point for a broader protectionist stand to save the surrounding wilderness from clear-cut logging operations. One of my duties included a guiding trek up the mountain with an assemblage of environmentalists, media personalities, local government officials, and representatives from the Teme-Augama Anishnabe reserve.

It was one of those dog days in mid-summer when you sweated profusely even while sitting motionless in the shade. Everyone collected at the old ranger's cabin at the base of the mountain, four kilometres from the summit. My trail crew had already cleared the old fire tower trail and built boardwalk and bridges across the bog holes; still, the climb was legend amongst canoeists — steep, precipitous inclines and a steady one-thousand vertical foot ascent to the apex.

The newly formed Preservation of the Lady Evelyn Wilderness Committee organized the event and had invited one of Ontario's most reputable environmental groups, represented by a thick-bearded executive director. It was a tough walk for many. Hot, constant uphill, rock-strewn slopes, biting flies; water bottles were empty by the time we reached the top of the mountain. Luckily, there was a water spring at the top, once used by the fire tower rangers. I was with a handful of dehydrated hikers, first to get to the summit, and we headed straight for the spring, located a couple hundred metres past the tower. It was covered with a piece of plywood to keep animals out of it and birds from shitting in it as they perched in the trees above. To keep the silt on the bottom from getting stirred up, you had to dip your cup carefully in the still water. But before anyone could fill their cups with clear, clean water, the environmentalist broke through the bevy of parched trekkers, fell to his knees, and stuck his hairy, sweaty, bearded head deep into the cool spring. He retreated quickly after filling his cup, still catching his breath and waving at the flies, moaning about how hard the climb was. Nobody said anything. We all waited for the water in the spring to settle; someone skimmed the hair out of the disturbed pool while others preferred to go thirsty. Quick speeches were made, some left tobacco as an offering, and the bearded eco-warrior had already headed back down the mountain.

Why I'm relating this story is critical to how I personally envisioned life as a green crusader. Champions of the wilderness, I thought, would be gallant, self-sacrificing and noble individuals. The social revolution already had its heroes deeply wedged into the psyche of North Americans. Canada had Greenpeace — spearheaded by writer Bob Hunter and activist Paul Watson; and in the States, Edward Abbey's book, "The Monkey Wrench Gang" — a how-to book for would-be saboteurs — spawned the formation of the direct action environmental group, Earth First!, under the tutelage of Dave Foreman and Mike Roselle. But the egoistic antics of the bearded enviro guy — *the jerk* — confounded my perception of green guardians; in fact, over the years I was to come to the realization that there were more zealots, monomaniacs, fanatics, and hedonists within the green movement than I would encounter either within the industrial or the bureaucratic authority. Plunderers of the green Earth know exactly what they want and the means to which they will go to obtain it. Their motives are clear-cut and money-driven. Environmentalists, on the other hand, whose intentions are more cryptic and symbolic, are motivated by passion, often to the point where they lose sight of reality.

Not to completely trash the green movement, but it functions primarily as a consciousness monitor — to prompt us to keep taking our blue box to the curb for pickup. I have lost my faith in the mainstream movement as they tend to compromise away the very wild lands the in-your-face environmentalists work so hard to protect. And this happens because the green leaders want to remain affable and polite in the eyes of the wolves — they don't want to be eaten up in the process. Process bogs them down in boardroom parley until they give in. Drawn out negotiations are simply industrial stall tactics, but ... we need the mainstreamers to lend credibility to the movement, chiefly because Canadians are polite, obliging people and they'd sooner open their wallets to respectful, non-confrontational canvassers.

But, what about the other part of the movement ... the "direct-action" advocates, front-liners, and monkey-wrenchers? Even Greenpeace has backed off from their action tactics — one reason why co-founder Paul Watson formed his own break-away group, The Sea Shepherd Society, now based out of Los Angeles. Watson realized that direct action could have far better results than polite debate. Direct action is a more radical form of civil disobedience and is wholly dependent on media for its success. It goes a step further than *symbolic action* (banners and protests) and its directive is to inflict enough economic damage so the company retreats (from mining, road building or logging, or factory fishing, whaling, etc.). Tree-spiking and trashing heavy equipment by putting rice in their radiators or sand in their gas tanks can be considered common practices of ecotage. Authorities tend to criminalize ecotage by branding it as a modern form of terrorism. According to the FBI, since 1996 there have been over six hundred incidents of domestic "terrorism" perpetrated by the Earth Liberation Front, or ELF, where arson is used to debilitate industrial activities in wilderness areas. Individuals who engage in environmental sabotage activities can claim them on behalf of the ELF if they meet three guidelines: (1) To inflict maximum economic damage on those profiting from the destruction and exploitation of the natural environment; (2) To reveal to, and to educate, the public about the atrocities committed against the Earth and all species that populate it; and (3) To take all necessary precautions against harming life. To date, no one has been injured or killed in any of these actions.

Jim Flynn, an Oregon-based environmentalist, in a 2007 *USA Today* article says: "I think that's really what all these actions are about, is really getting public attention to some of these issues … if we were able to affect policy change through more legal means, then certainly that's the way these people would go. Nobody enjoys being underground, and that lifestyle."

Ecotage works and the authorities are unwilling to admit it. They can't, because there would be a total breakdown of the system of order. The politics of wilderness (and wilderness is now considered a valuable commodity because of its scarcity) demand a stringent adherence to management doctrines, as one-sided as they may be toward industry. Allowing the armour to be chinked could crash the guiding principles of a multi-use objective. It would also give credence to the viability of the left-wing fringe environmental movement. Paranoia is the reason why the establishment has come down hard on the perpetrators, setting higher penalties for green crimes. In Marin County, California, three enviro-crusaders were arrested and sentenced to one year in jail and a total of fifty-thousand dollars in fines. Granted, these were serious actions against public and private property. In the United States, the FBI has clustered the granola-munching green activist with the bonified gun-wielding terrorist in an attempt to make any threat against homeland security one and the same as far as the law is concerned. The fixation on "terror-isms" that is rampant in the States is not quite as apparent in Canada, probably because we lack the proliferation of cult followings and radical left-wing green earth crusaders. We're just nice people.

One form of ecotage that has had proven results worldwide is the construction of illegal trails; trails usually built on public land owned by the state or province and, in most cases, through a tract of land that may be threatened by development. The emphasis here is to attract people to the location, encouraging them to participate in a particular issue; and if enough people flock to the newly hacked out trail, their collective letters and complaints to the local administration just might be enough to halt plans for logging or mining.

In Temagami, while I was mapping out the canoe routes for the government guidebook, I also included upgrades on all the historic fire tower trails. The strategy behind this was to get canoeists off the water routes and onto land-based trails where the protection of viewscapes could be included in the master plan ... much to the chagrin of local foresters whose old arguments in favour of clear-cuts to the shoreline was founded on the fact that paddlers never stray far from the water trails. During my tenure as interior ranger, I was privy to the district timber planning operations; whenever there was a proposed logging cut near or within a sensitive area, I would chart out and propose a hiking trail in that same block of land. In the past, if there were no objections or conflicts of use within a proposed cutting area, industry had carte blanche treatment. But propose a hiking trail that would increase tourist flow, and get the scheme into the system files, and you could successfully block the intent by industry to log or build roads in that area.

For me it was a clandestine, albeit dogmatic, approach to solving a problem in the system. I had a night key to the district office and I would forage through master plans and timber allocation maps in the middle of the night. Of the four proposed trails I managed to insert into the planning process, three trails came to fruition. In 1980, I diverted my portage crew to work on the Temagami Island trail system where local logging companies wanted access to one of Ontario's most magnificent stands of old-growth red and white pine. Once the trail was established, the people came, and they walked through a forest they would not normally have the opportunity to see up close. The existence of the trail created its own lobby group. Although this was a legally sanctioned trail, the means in which it was conceived could be construed as under-handed and coerced.

Deeper into the Temagami wild lands is the Wakimika Triangle — a lush, sweeping forest of gargantuan pine trees, precipitous escarpments, and clear-water lakes. It's one of North America's largest remaining stands of old-growth red and white pine. Logging companies have been tripping over each other to get in there and cut it down. A timber access road was pushed north into its sacred domain, a bridge was built over the Obabika River and the Wakimika forest was in sight. While this was happening, our newly founded environmental group, the Temagami Wilderness Society, or TWS (now Earthroots), had been building hiking trails within the forest. This is an illegal activity on Crown property; however, it was sanctioned by the local Ojibwa family, the Misabe's, whose traditional homeland included the Wakimika forest. At the same time, tree-spikers riddled the big pines at the terminus of the logging road (and beyond) with twelve-inch steel spikes, rendering the pine stands unmarketable. This was an act not carried out by the TWS for obvious reasons; their mandate was to get people walking the newly constructed old-growth trails in order to bolster support for the issue. This was too much, too fast, for the local forestry office to handle, and in Ontario, nobody had yet to be charged with building illegal trails, or fined for spiking trees. It was also too much for the logging companies to deal with: the bridge had been burned out, trees were spiked, and it wasn't worth taking a chance running trees through the mill band saw, or for sawyers to cut down the trees with the chance of hitting a nail. The media dragged the local Natural Resources administration through the mud, pulverizing them in every major newspaper in Canada. In the end, the Wakimika Triangle, including the section of spiked forest, was indoctrinated into the park system.

As a side note, tree-spiking was first initiated to save forests in the 1800s, and then popularized in Dave Foreman's (co-founder of Earth First!) book, *EcoDefense*. According to the Association of Oregon Loggers, "the average ecotage incident costs $60,000 in equipment loss and downtime." And that's exactly what tree-spikers aspire to achieve — to make the venture for the company unprofitable. In British Columbia, Meares Island was slotted for clear-cutting, but it was cancelled after extensive and well planned tree-spiking.

Does tree-spiking harm the trees? Not according to University of Maine biologist Jonathan Carter who did extensive studies on the subject: "Unless copper is used, steel and ceramic spikes will not harm trees."

Many environmentalists feel that they have been put in a position where there is no longer any legal control over the issue and the only remaining options are those outside the law. The question remains: Does tree-spiking work? Some companies will engage workers in a spike removal operation using a metal detector and crowbar. This in itself is costly for the company and it gets to the point where they have to determine if the value of the trees is worth the effort. If I were a tree-spiker, this is what I would do:

1) Make sure the stand of trees is actually slated for logging. Timber allocation maps are usually prepared a year or two in advance of the proposed cut and available to the public. Get somebody not involved in the field work to acquire maps. You don't want to waste your time spiking a forest that isn't on the hit list.

2) Plan the operation well in advance of the actual cut. Some companies will position motion detectors and video cameras along roads, bridges, and within the stand itself nearing the time of operations. Plan alternative means of access and avoid roads and peak forest-use seasons.

3) Have someone else purchase spikes, or devise a surrogate project like deck-building, retaining wall, or any reason why you would purchase spikes. Cut off the heads so they can't be pulled out of the trees or use rebar cut in ten-inch lengths. Ceramic spikes are also becoming popular, as metal detectors can't locate them.

4) Clean your work area thoroughly. A six-month investigation by state conservation officers and the FBI traced tree-spiking nails to Frank Ambrose, twenty-six, an affiliate of the ELF, through hardware store surveillance tapes. His car was also spotted near the forest at the time of the incident, and police found hammering and metal-cutting tools and cotton gloves with a residue similar to that from the spikes in Ambrose's apartment.

5) Sink the nails past the bark line so that the protective sap layer covers the spike and is more difficult to extricate. Use tree-climbers (spiked foot harnesses used by arborists and linesmen) or a ladder to pound nails in at higher levels.

6) Always use gloves and leave no trace.
7) Carefully inform the authorities of the exact location of the spiked forest well in advance of any intrusive road building or logging.

Illegal trail building can do harm to the environment if not carefully executed. Mountain bike enthusiasts are notorious for building new trails on private or government lands and are often caught, punished accordingly, and the trails removed. These ventures are usually self-serving with no intent to help save an area from development. Well planned and conceived hiking trails, including water trails or canoe routes, work favourably in garnishing public support. However, a poorly constructed trail can have a rebound effect if improperly established. Portage trails need to be carefully scrutinized for historic or cultural importance and cleared accordingly. New hiking trails must also conform to the doctrines of sustainable trail-building techniques: avoiding fall-line or steep inclines where runoff may occur; avoiding cutting trees more than four inches in diameter; and avoiding sensitive flora and fauna. If an illegal trail conforms to proper trail construction methodology and there is no harm done to the ecological integrity, the local forestry office has less of a case against the perpetrator. Trail construction should be done in the off-season with the employment of hand tools only. On average, two seasoned trailbuilders can construct five hundred to a thousand metres of trail in a day's work using nothing more than a Pulaski (a single-bit axe with an adze-shaped hoe extending from the back), loppers, and rake. The pay is lousy but the associated benefits are enormous.

River sculpture — the art of misfortune.

Wrecked Canoe on Stump by Hap Wilson.

PART TWO
JOURNEY'S END:
SIX WAYS TO DIE ON THE TRAIL

One can survive everything, nowadays, except death, and live down everything except a good reputation.
— Oscar Wilde (1854–1900)

There are many more ways to live in the wilderness, comfortably and secure, than there are ways to die. The abruptness of tragedy along the trail compels us to be more wary. Wilderness is not the arena in which you always learn from your mistakes. And mistakes are not patented by the uninitiated or foolish alone; they are often perpetrated by seasoned adventurers who should know better. The section titled *Journey's End* purposely extracts all that is good about the adventure; the intrinsic pristine beauty of the landscape, the friendly camaraderie, the experience, and replaces it with the unmasked realities of life along the trail. It is not with the intention of dissuading the adventure-seeker from embarking on a journey, but to make him aware of the ease in which misadventure may take hold if unprepared. Living comfortably and peacefully in the wilds depends on a reliance of accrued knowledge, accepting all and any possibilities, and being humble in the face of Nature.

What we don't know will hurt us.

Spirit Water by Hap Wilson.

SIX
HYPOTHERMIA

Iron rusts from disuse; stagnant water loses its purity and in cold weather becomes frozen; even so does inaction sap the vigour of the mind.

— Leonardo da Vinci (1452–1519)

You start to shiver, sporadically at first, but then uncontrollably. Hands become numb and it's difficult to take the lens cap off your camera. Goosebumps form over your entire body it seems as your breathing becomes quick and shallow. Shivering is violent now and any movements are slow and laboured. You stumble and your hat falls off but you don't pick it up. Lips are pale. Ears, fingers, and toes are turning blue. Suddenly you feel this warm sensation and the shivering stops but you have trouble speaking. Your hands remain limp at your sides but you stagger on. You forget where you are and where you are going. Exposed skin becomes blue and puffy. There is some comfort as you lie down on the wet ground. Breathing slows as you drift off. Half an hour later your heart stops.

Hypothermia can occur in the summer; most people don't realize this. Parents watch as their children swim off the dock at the cottage. Within fifteen minutes their lips are blue and they're shivering uncontrollably. They wrap towels around them and tell them to sit in the sun or put clothes on. What parents don't know is that little Johnny's core temperature has dropped two degrees Celsius, from the normal thirty-seven degrees down to thirty-five degrees. That doesn't seem like much but when the body temperature drops below thirty degrees, all major organs fail and clinical death occurs.

Hypothermia, or what was once referred to as "exposure," is the number one killer in the outdoor adventure trade. And it happens a lot, mostly because people are unprepared or inexperienced. The unprepared tend to die on the trail, whereas the inexperienced die in the water. Either way, death by hypothermia, in most cases, is preventable.

I have been close to death more times than I would like to admit to. And I have been so cold and wet and miserable and tired that all I wanted to do was to lie down and sleep. But my will and instinct to survive overrode any self-doubt and I managed to pull myself from the edge each time, perhaps a little smarter for the experience. And most of these affairs occurred when I was younger and I brandished an imperishable attitude. I fought Nature on my terms alone; it was a constant battle to survive because I had yet to learn how to *live* within the dictates of the natural world. It's much different now, and as a wilderness guide I have the welfare of the client to consider ... and the client constantly tests your ability to ameliorate situations.

One of the odd dichotomies about wilderness guiding is the tenets governing the well-being of the guide. The guide remains, at all times, stoic, gallant, and self-sacrificing, which is true to an extent. But there are times when the guide is vulnerable, mostly due to his or her actions while tending client needs. On whitewater river trips, particularly in the Far North where water and air temperatures often hover just above freezing, it is often difficult to remain dry. The guide is in and out of the water or weather constantly — dislodging canoes off rocks, fixing equipment, pitching camp — while relentlessly checking the well-being of the group, and Gore-Tex jackets get thoroughly soaked inside from sweat and outside from rain or snow. During these times I have felt myself slipping into the first stages of hypothermia, well knowing the consequences should I allow it to progress to the point where I can no longer make a rational decision, or carry out even basic tasks. At this juncture there are few options. It is here that my own welfare supplants that of the client and the decision is made to stop, erect a temporary weather shelter, make a fire, brew a pot of tea, and get out of wet clothes. I am the first to tend to my needs. Usually by this point others in the group are also in need of a warm-up. The guide cannot benefit the group if debilitated; it's the same principle extolled while flying in a jet with your children — you are always instructed to put on your own oxygen mask before assisting your kids.

I was hired one winter to guide and instruct a large group of high-school students who were stationed at a well-known outdoor school. The directors had assured me that all students had been well-trained in basic winter survival skills. Our destination was Temagami where we would trek in and set up a base camp using large canvas prospector tents equipped with wood stoves. It had snowed heavily overnight but the temperature hovered just above freezing and the snow was wet and sticky. I had instructed everyone not to bring skis because the conditions warranted travel by snowshoe. When I arrived at the base camp it was raining, the buses were parked and waiting, but the students were all standing out in the weather without their outer gear on — the instructors were nowhere to be seen. Thoroughly soaked, the students then sat in the heated bus for three hours for the ride to our start point. When they unloaded the bus there were no snowshoes — just skis; to add to the complexity of the expedition, one of the leaders had a severe cold. By the time we had everyone harnessed to their respective toboggans it was mid-afternoon and it would be dark by the time we arrived at our prospective campsite. The snow stuck to the bottoms of the skis like cement, everyone was cold from the start, and progress was interminably slow. I dropped my own load several times and went up and down the line encouraging the students (and leaders) to keep moving until we reached the campsite. Fortunately, I had brought a large thermos of coffee which was rationed out to the neediest along the line. I broke a trail to the campsite and began excavating a spot for one of the tents and gathered enough firewood to last a couple of hours. The group was in a sad state by the time they reached the campsite and few were able to carry out chores with any efficiency. We set up the one tent and ignited a fire in the stove and everyone huddled inside to get warm. This could have been a routine winter camping expedition with no hitches; instead, the directors of the group were negligent in preparing the group for the outing. The students were also incapable of setting up camp and lighting fires with any proficiency, even after I was told by the staff that they had already received extensive training.

One of the inherent mistakes made by winter trekkers and often those in a leadership capacity is to treat a winter expedition like a summer trip. A summer kilometre is two or three in the winter if the conditions are bad, and those beautiful summer campsites on the lake could be a winter camper's nemesis during a storm. Judging the distance you can walk on snowshoes pulling a toboggan, or skiing with a backpack in the winter is more difficult, especially travelling with a large group. Students are notorious for not dressing appropriately and they often don't factor in the consequences; to them, rescue is always close at hand, until something happens and the reality that they are in the wilderness sinks in.

One of the classic cases of a mismanaged expedition was the Lake Temiskaming tragedy of 1978. It was my first year as a ranger and the headwater of the Ottawa River was in my jurisdiction. I had paddled down this wide section of river on two occasions before; it was legend amongst the residents of the established canoe camps on Lake Temagami who made the crossing regularly, that this body of water was to be respected. On June 11, the St. John's School headed out with thirty-one paddlers in four brand new canoes. They were eighteen-footers, not quite freighter or voyageur canoes, the leaders put eight in three canoes and seven in the other. Overloaded, the boats laboured in the rough waters. One canoe swamped, and then a second that went to help the first, then a third canoe went over. The fourth canoe did its best to shuttle kids and teachers to the Ontario side of the river but it wasn't enough to save twelve kids, aged ten to fifteen, and one teacher. The river water temperature was seven degrees Celsius; a body loses heat twenty-five times faster submersed in water than on land. The kids never survived much more than an hour before succumbing to hypothermia.

St. John's School of Ontario was an Anglican boys' school whose tenets supported corporal punishment; students were to endure pain and hardship to develop stronger character. Since the accident there have been several documents produced, critiquing the misguided expedition, including James Raffan's book *Deep Waters*, published in 2002. And through my own experiences as a park ranger and guide, having observed school and church groups in the wilds, there are obvious logical conclusions we critics can hypothesize about the tragedy: that the guides (or teachers) made fatal decisions based on their collective inexperience in big water crossings. I'm surprised that there haven't been more accidents like this one. Proper jurisprudence by the guide/teacher would have included a risk management strategy that included precautions travelling over large bodies of cold water. On my trips I'll raft two or more canoes together to make crossings or run big rapids that can be kilometres long. Dumping on big lakes or on long rapids can be tough to remedy, not to mention life-threatening. In 2004, there were twenty-three canoe-related deaths and three kayak-related deaths in Canada.

The modern body of medical knowledge — a clearly ethical issue — about how the human body reacts to freezing to the point of death is based almost exclusively on experiments carried out in 1941 by the Nazis in Germany. The Luftwaffe conducted experiments on prisoners to learn how to treat hypothermia. One study forced subjects to endure a tank of ice water for up to three hours; another study placed prisoners naked in the open for several hours with temperatures below freezing. The experiments assessed different ways of re-warming survivors. These morbid tests were carried out by the Nazi High Command at Dachau and Auschwitz, selections made of young healthy Jews or Russians. The experiments were conducted on men to simulate the conditions the armies suffered on the Eastern Front, as the German forces were ill-prepared for the bitter cold. The two-part freezing experiments established how long it would take to lower the body temperature to death, and how to best resuscitate the frozen victim. Test subjects were usually stripped naked for the experiment. An insulated probe which measured the drop in body temperature was inserted into the rectum and held in place by an expandable metal ring which was adjusted to open inside the rectum to hold the probe firmly in place. The victim was put into an air force uniform, then placed in a vat of cold ice-water and allowed to freeze.

One of the regular occurrences I've come across in the Far North where hypothermic conditions have no seasonal boundaries is *paradoxical undressing*. Almost 50 percent of hypothermic deaths are associated with this phenomenon. It typically occurs during moderate to severe hypothermia where the victim becomes disoriented, confused, and combative. The victim may begin discarding clothing, like mitts or hats or even overcoats, which in turn increases the rate of temperature loss. There have been several documented case studies of victims throwing off their clothes before help reached them.

A late, good friend of mine, Victoria Jason, in her book *Kabloona in the Yellow Kayak* describes her adventure up the coast of Hudson Bay with explorer Don Starkle. Starkle ranks with other Canadian adventurers, like John Hornby, who pushed their limits well past their ability or knowledge to survive. Starkle sat in his kayak in a hypothermic state, in sight of rescue, but had removed his mitts which allowed his fingers to freeze solid.

On Arctic canoeing expeditions, where inclement weather and wind conditions prevail and clients often get wet, hypothermia is a constant concern. The guide is subject to wet conditions, always, on shallow rivers where clients continually get hung up on rocks and need to be assisted. There is often no shelter except for the tent which is pitched at the end of a day. Clothing, damp from sweat inside, or soaked through by snow and rain, waterlogged boots, and general malaise and flailing spirit, all add up and can easily culminate in a serious hypothermia climax. To say I've had tough days on the trail is an understatement; clients need constant attention, beyond the needs of the guide, and there have been occasional circumstances where I've had to rescue cast-off clothing, hats, gloves, vests, and even lifejackets — all the things necessary and critical in keeping someone warm even though everything may be damp. Paradoxical undressing can happen even at the onset of mild hypothermia: when an objective destination is set, and circumstances arise when it is best to just keep moving until adequate shelter can be secured, clients (and some inexperienced guides) get careless. Even though they know they dropped something, in their faltering mind it makes sense to forget about it, however irrational and dangerous, they plod on with a false sensation of warmth, or the anticipation of getting to a warm place soon. There have been many situations when it was necessary to stop where there was no lee-cover from the wind, set up a makeshift shelter using canoes and brew a pot of tea, simply because one client showed signs of hypothermia. Clients can only be pushed as far as the weakest member; physical and psychological conditioning has a breaking point — going beyond this point compromises the integrity of the trip and the safety of the group. Unguided, inexperienced groups generally rely on the strongest (or most vocal) member of the party if situations arise. Selecting a leader this way is a slipshod method of maintaining stability and duty of care, especially knowing that human nature casts most of us as sheep. One person slipping into a hypothermic state can spell quick disaster for a group if it is not remedied quickly; once a person hits the second and third stage of cold immersion it gets harder to bring them back and easier for the rescuer to cause the victim to succumb to cardiac arrest while trying desperately to warm them up. Tricks and back-pocket remedies found in "survival" manuals are futile when common sense has been abandoned.

Moisture is the bane of the adventurer's peaceful existence. I hate being wet and I'll do anything to stay as dry as possible. I have no qualms about pitching a good kitchen tarp over a firepit on a rainy day, cooking, reading, and watching other canoeists or hikers passing through, miserable and wet. There have been many occasions when the smell of fresh-brewed coffee and sweet-buns baked in the reflector oven has attracted the appearance of sodden campers who appreciate getting in out of the rain and drying out, if only for a temporary stopover.

While acting as a guest park warden in New Zealand, tending a forty-eight-bunk hut along the Routeburn Track in Aspiring National Park, I was amazed to see how poorly many of the hikers were dressed. I was there for the month of May, at the onset of the New Zealand winter, and a time when the tail end of the hiking season still attracted enough trampers to warrant keeping the warden's hut open. People would arrive after the hard climb to the hut, often soaked from sweat, wearing nothing more than tight blue jeans and sneakers and perhaps a light wind-shell. In the Southern Alps of the park, the climate changes from balmy warm in the lush valleys to bitter cold up in the treeless passes. Several people had died along this track, either from venturing off the trail and succumbing to hypothermia, or by slipping off the icy edge of a trail along a mountain pass. I spent most of my time keeping a warming fire going in the bunkhouse, lending trampers adequate clothing (which was returned on the trek back), or moderating the effects of hypothermia on ill-prepared hikers. A young man from Quebec had left his pack, bedroll, and food at the terminus of the trail, fifteen kilometres away, and had made his way to my hut over one of the mountain ridges. By the time he arrived at the Routeburn Falls hut he was hypothermic but insisted on walking the fifteen kilometres back to his gear along the trail. I refused to let him go and he stayed in my cabin for two days drying out and shaking off a deadly chill. He was physically fit and an ardent trekker, but he lacked the ability to pace himself or to judge how far he could travel in unknown territory.

SEVEN
ERRANT MAPS

One should not take every map that comes out, upon trust, or conclude that the newest is still the best, but ought to be at pains to examine them by the observations of the best travelers, that he may know their goodness and defects.

— John Green, *The Construction of Maps and Globes*, 1717

After looking at the topographic map, the four Ohio paddlers decided to continue along the east side of the rapids approaching Thunderhouse Falls to see if they could locate the portage. At the time, they had no idea that the portage marked on the map did not exist, and by the time they noticed canoeists across the river, unloading their gear at the trailhead upstream, it was too late. Craig Zelenak, 33, and his canoe partner, Pat Sirk, 32, would later describe the power of the rapids as a "roller coaster ride with three-foot waves all around." In an attempt to cross over to the other side of the river and work their way up to the portage, both canoes capsized. Zelenak and Sirk made it back to shore, but for their friends in the other canoe, Ken Randlett, 39, and David Zenisek, 23, the flow of the current was too much.

The four Cleveland-area companions spent weekends and holidays together, usually canoeing, and to them, a trip down the Missinaibi River

The trail is marked by purpose, not by signage.

was to be a trip of a lifetime. Randlett, who planned to spend his fortieth birthday on the river, spent a year organizing the expedition; Zenisek was to be married shortly after their return. The last Zelenak and Sirk saw of their friends, the two of them were clinging to the canoe and heading for the falls. They were both wearing lifejackets so they figured they would be okay.

A group of Canadian canoeists had congregated at the campsite overlooking the gorge, some distance along the sixteen-hundred-metre portage. They were in the process of portaging their gear and were now taking a few restful minutes absorbing the spectacular scene below them — the thunderous applause of a great river squeezed between ancient ramparts of granite. They had no idea of the tragedy unfolding above the falls at that moment. Walking casually along the brim of the canyon, the Canadians came in sight of the first chute, still dazzled by the immensity of the spillway and the gallery of water-worn rocks. They soon saw that something was definitely out of place; the prow of a canoe bobbed up and down in the surging pool between the first two chutes, a lifejacket ripped in half, a pack and a plastic cooler remained partly visible, caught in a boil of aerated water and river foam. Two of the Canadians had already gone back to the head of the portage where they soon met up with the remaining half of the Ohio party who still believed their friends had made it to shore safely, maybe mingling with the Canadians down at the campsite. The utter horror of the situation sank in when they discovered that their friends were unaccounted for, and that the mangled canoe and torn lifejacket had turned up at the bottom of the falls. *They were all wearing lifejackets*, Zelenak thought aloud.

A frenzied shore search resulted in little hope of finding anyone alive.

On June 21, 1993, the Rescue Co-ordination Centre in Trenton, Ontario, responded to an activated Emergency Locating Transmitter (E.L.T.) on the Missinaibi River, almost a thousand kilometres to the north. An Ontario Provincial Police Search and Rescue Team and helicopter were dispatched early the following day and made contact with a group of paddlers camped at Thunderhouse Falls. Four days later, the rescue team located one of the bodies in Bell's Bay, twenty-four kilometres downstream from Thunderhouse. The second body was found the next day just below Conjuring House Rapids.

Twenty-five days later, provincial police and Natural Resources officials met in Hearst with local coroner, Bertrand Proulx. Proulx had recalled a similar drowning some years earlier at Thunderhouse but did not want to call an inquest because of the expense, according to the records of the meeting. The report adds, "… especially when he knows what the inquest's recommendations would be, anyways." There was no mention in any of the records to making any effort to correct the false information on the topographic map that had led the Ohio party astray.

At the time I was writing a canoeing guidebook to the Missinaibi River, initially because it was both a provincial waterway park and a Canadian Heritage River. The scope of the book changed when I heard about the recent drownings at Thunderhouse. I was on the river at the time, near the headwater, and heard about the tragedy in the riverside village of Mattice while picking up supplies. Two days later I was camped at Thunderhouse, trying to picture what had happened to the Ohio men. Beaching my canoe below the falls and canyon, I hiked up to the pool where the non-existent portage was marked on the map — the portage the Ohio men tried to reach. The pool near where I was standing (where the portage was supposed to be) was relatively calm, streaked with river foam and slowly recirculating; the rapid entering the pool was dramatic and tightly wound with a sharp decline toward the first falls. *Even a good, strong paddler could not exit the rapids and get across the pond safely here*, I thought. My eye caught a flash of sunlight from an object pushed up along the shore rocks. It was a waterproof, disposable camera, probably belonging to the Ohio men that dumped in the rapids. It was a strange feeling to be holding the record of the last hours of the two dead men in my hand.

A year earlier I was paddling the upper Missinaibi with a girlfriend and had pulled over at an open bedrock island in the middle of Albany Rapids for lunch. A Search and Rescue helicopter landed a quarter of a kilometre downstream and unloaded several men and a small boat. We thought this was just a training exercise. Packing up, we pushed on, paddling the rapid in front of the SAR group and exchanging casual waves.

When we reached Mattice and dropped in to sign the river guestbook at Nancy's restaurant, owner Doris Tanguay mentioned that someone had drowned upriver at Albany Rapids about a week ago and that the rescue squad was having difficulty getting the body out of the river. I realized we had paddled directly over a dead man that was wedged in rocks underwater and that the SAR members we had passed were still trying to extricate the body. The log book showed that over a hundred paddlers had passed through in the last four days, and they, too, had paddled over the body in the rapids.

After the two Thunderhouse drownings and the one at Albany Rapids, I was beginning to wonder if there was a trend or pattern to the deaths. I was also curious to see if there were any other deaths along the river in the past years. I was already suspecting inaccuracies with the topographic maps and well knew their faults and failures, but I wanted to find out if any other deaths had been the cause of errant maps. I had appealed to the Natural Resources regional office for funding for my research and was turned down, but I was determined to continue my investigations.

Requesting the appropriate access to information documents, I was finally approved and allowed to visit the Ontario Coroner's Office in Toronto. I was given a cubicle and instructions how to use their filing system. I'd search back to 1977, or seventeen years of records, and isolate only those boating deaths that had occurred anywhere along the Missinaibi River Heritage route, from Lake Superior to Moosonee on James Bay — a total distance of about 650 kilometres. It was a daunting task, time consuming and unsettling. For the next three days I would leaf through over five hundred police and coroner reports, isolating all the deaths that had occurred along one Canadian river system. Thankfully, there were no photographs in the reports, except in the last file I examined. Leafing through a file dated June 1981, two crisp glossy photographs flipped out on to the table. My stomach lurched at what I saw. I took in a deep breath and stared at the pictures. I couldn't take my eyes off them. There were two young men, obviously dead, stretched unceremoniously on stainless-steel gurneys — a morgue photo. Both still had their lifejackets on. The cold water of the Missinaibi had preserved their bodies, at least from bloating, but their skin was bleach white, eyes vacant and darkened by death. The whiteness of their skin accentuated cuts, contusions, and fractures; broken necks, crushed skulls, limbs twisted out of symmetry. One dead youth was wearing my brand of lifejacket with extrication knife attached. It was weird; when I first saw the picture it was like I was looking at myself, dead. Both young men were twenty-three years old, from Brooklyn, New York, and had belonged to a whitewater paddling club. They were experienced paddlers. There were four in the party; the survivors reported that their friends had been "sucked" into the rapids and couldn't get out of the pull to the falls. They were headed for a non-existent portage, just as the Ohio men had done. It was the very last of the five hundred files. I quickly packed up my research material and left the building. I found a quiet park bench and sat down and wept, deep sobs, for the parents of these boys who were probably spared the pictures I had just seen. Then I got angry.

It was even hard writing about this incident fourteen years later without feeling emotionally charged. There had been thirty-five drownings in the time period I had researched, or an average of about two deaths per year. Eleven of those deaths occurred within the boundaries of the Missinaibi Provincial and Heritage Waterway Park; twelve of the drownings, about one-third of the total, were American tourists. Seventeen of the drownings could have been prevented. Five died at Thunderhouse Falls because the topographic map told them to portage at a spot on the river that was virtually impossible to access. Twelve of the sixteen Federal topographic maps covering the river corridor had gross errors. Thirty-five of the ninety-three rapids were unmarked and two dangerous falls were not on the maps at all. Twelve portages were missing and six were marked in the wrong location. I had chosen the figure of seventeen years of research into the deaths because it backdated events to the last map update in 1978. Ontario Hydro at that time had plans of building a dam at Thunderhouse Falls and the topographic map had needed updating for official proposed plans. I interviewed the librarian at Western University's research facility. She actually knew of the incident where government cartographers had argued over where to insert the portage on the Thunderhouse map. It was arbitrarily affixed to the map at what looked like the shortest route around the falls. Since the map was from a series of "white" sheets, any correction done would now show up highlighted in purple on the black and white maps. The Canada Map Office produces 12,150 of the popular 1:50,000 scale topographic maps most widely used by adventurers — ninety percent of the charts cover "undeveloped" regions above the so-called "wilderness-line," and are in dire need of revisions, particularly along rivers having park or heritage status.

During the winter of 1993–94, I retreated to a cabin on Lake Superior to write my book. The research was unsettling. I appealed to the provincial coroner, James G. Young, to call for an inquest into the high number of deaths linked to poor maps and misleading advertising by both the provincial and federal governments. I had interviewed Peter Andrews from the Canada Map Office in Ottawa and was told that "... we (Energy Mines and Resources) don't recommend that canoeists use just the topographic maps for reference." Andrews also stated that EMR would never advertise in a strictly canoeing or outdoor magazine; however, their full-page "All roads lead to roam" ad, a crowing statement that EMR maps "will lead you in the right direction," did, in fact, find its way into Canada's national canoeing magazine, *Kanawa*, and other American adventure-oriented magazines, as well. The Ontario Tourism Ministry had just spent close to $100,000 on splashy full-page, colour ads in American magazines touting the Missinaibi as a Heritage River you could paddle from start to finish, across the breadth of Ontario, and cross only two roads — the same year the two men from Ohio died at Thunderhouse Falls. Many provincial and federal departments aggressively market to back-country travellers, pitching Canadian wilderness, a product the bureaucrats know very little about. Ad hype and hastily packaged materials continue to lure adventurers to provincial parks and remote rivers.

The Canadian Federal Department of Indian and Northern Affairs "Wild River Survey" was carried out in 1971–73, in which sixty-five rivers across Canada were surveyed for recreational potential. Mike Greco, past secretariat of the Canadian Heritage River Board and Foundation says of the survey:

"… the ten published booklets, although available to the public, were never intended for navigational purposes … some were withdrawn because of inaccuracies — mishaps were occurring, especially in British Columbia because much of the compiled information wasn't field-truthed … anyone canoeing in remote regions should be extra careful using 1:50,000 maps and avail themselves of any professional literature before heading out."

Legal counsellor for the Canadian Recreational Canoeing Association, John Eberhard, had told me that "canoeists may have cause for legal action against both the provincial and federal governments determining the lack of 'duty of care' in producing public material, including topographical maps…." Six months had passed since the Ohio deaths, a lapse of too much time to initiate legal action by the family. I had the photographs developed from the camera I had found floating in the pool at Thunderhouse — just a tight group of fun-loving guys having a great time without a care in the world.

I called Brian McAndrew, the environment reporter for the *Toronto Star* newspaper, and told him about the research I was doing. Within twenty-four hours he was on a plane for Sault Ste. Marie where I would pick him up in my truck and bring him north to Michipicoten, where my cabin was. The feature front-page story on May 8, 1994, read: "When a line on a canoeists' map spells death at Thunderhouse Falls."

McAndrew later told me that the story had provoked more phone calls and letters than he had ever received for any story he had written. He was deluged with story after story about close calls and near-tragedies at Thunderhouse and elsewhere along the river, including one about four guys who actually survived going over the falls in a rubber raft.

The Natural Resources provincial office called me shortly after the release of the story and offered to contribute $10,000 to my research costs. It was also agreed that proper warning signs would be erected at Mattice and on an island before the Thunderhouse portage. The faulty topographical sheet was temporarily removed from Federal stock, pending updates scheduled in the future.

The rhetorical question here is, "Who is at fault?" The obvious problem is twofold: the Canadian government is not providing accurate technical information for backcountry canoe routes, specifically for highly publicized parks and Heritage Rivers; and the canoeing public puts too much faith in topographical charts — maps that were never intended for adventure-oriented recreation.

Long before the white man came to Canada, Native people were scratching crude maps in the sand or on rolls of birchbark. People of the First Nations had a "built-in" knowledge of place and distance and were often employed by early explorers as guides. Early maps etched out by John Cabot, Jacques Cartier, and John Davis did not survive; however, in 1604–08, Samuel de Champlain — zealot and cartographer — did give us eleven large-scale charts of eastern "Canada," drawn to indicate sovereignty over the land and resources therein. Canada was not an easy country to explore because of its vast, rugged topography, extreme environmental conditions, and short travelling season. But not just that, transferring information from a sphere to a flat plane involved advanced mathematics which worked only in open, unforested areas. Errors published on early maps remained uncorrected for centuries, chiefly because of the high cost of changing printing plates. Explorers, too, were not always proficient mapmakers so that a lot of "longitudinal" discrepancies were found in working charts well into the nineteenth century.

The Hudson's Bay Company's push for ever more furs prompted the need for more accurate maps of the interior and gave rise to the development of better survey instruments, tools used by the likes of Philip Turnor (1778–79), Sir Alexander Mackenzie (1789–93), and David Thompson and George Vancouver (1793). Much of Canada's shape and size was well-charted by the turn of the century, although northern Quebec and the Arctic islands remained a mystery.

The Geological Survey of Canada, founded in 1842, went through a period of changes, eventually to become the Topographical Surveys Branch formed in 1883. Burgeoning westward settlement in the United States may have rushed the surveying of Canada by often inexperienced field crews; maps produced in the early 1900s were "so inaccurate that the details were kept secret for 50 years" (Milliken Report). The

"Chief Cartographer's" series of maps, drawn to the 1:250,000 and 1:500,000 scale commenced in 1903. A year later the Survey Division of the Department of Militia and Defence was created with the intent to map all of Canada in the one-inch to one-mile scale (the scale popularized with outdoors people today). In 1902, the DMD had realized the importance of detailed maps during the Boer War. Canada, being short on cartographic savvy, hired R.H. Chapman of the U.S. Geological Survey in 1908 to try and shape up the topographic unit within its Canadian counterpart. There were now three uncoordinated departments producing maps. This continued until 1922, when the formation of the Board on Topographical Surveys and Maps was created to respond to the need for some kind of standardization. The BTS&M evolved into a division of Energy, Mines, and Resources in 1966 (EMR) and it continues to be known by that name today.

Acknowledged as the "map for all seasons," the one-inch to one-mile series was eventually converted to the popular 1:50,000 scale by photo-enlargement after 1950. By the 1930s, specific geographic areas of northern Canada were being mapped using "air-oblique" methods of range-finding, traverses down the more prominent rivers; methods deemed "sketchy" by the more advanced European cartographers. Photographs depicting water levels during high-flow could not detail many locations of rapids and falls, and consequently some of these discrepancies have not been corrected to this day. W.F. Phelan of the Geographic Survey remarked about pre-Second World War maps that "vagaries of water-courses beyond open-country could not be relied on, but on the whole there was little criticism by those who occasion to use these sheets."

By the late 1940s, photogrammetry (the science of drawing maps from air photos) improved with the use of "electronic distance measuring devices" or EDMs, where aerial photography now employed overlapping traverse patterns. Maps surveyed between 1945 and 1962, according to the Association of Canadian Map Librarians and Archives in Ottawa, are generally considered "the most inaccurate." This just happens to include maps covering the greater portion of the Canadian northland!

Today, the use of survey satellites measuring the "Doppler Shift" (change in frequency of sound, radio, or light waves) has improved map accuracy to within inches; that's great for physical discrepancies, but without information revisions, any updates would not improve maps for the paddler headed for a non-existent portage.

In 1956, the Canadian military found it urgent to map out the Arctic regions because of the mounting threat of nuclear war which would effectively put northern Canada directly between the major powers. These hastily produced maps were very basic and lacked any detail. In 1967, the six-colour map was introduced for "southern Canada," while the "Wilderness Line" demarked the use of black and white monochrome maps, thus making a clear distinction between settled and unsettled regions. Since the rate of development in the North is slow, revisions were not a priority and would take place every thirty years, unless, as in the case of Thunderhouse Falls, a major development is proposed. Urban maps would be revised every five years. EMR has recently changed their revision policy to every three years.

In 1994, I began my wild river survey research for the Province of Manitoba and Canada Parks, Heritage Rivers branch, which sponsored my first trip down the Seal River. Before any mapping expedition, I make an effort to obtain any current or archival published material and Canada Parks supplied what they had on public file. It wasn't until I was on the river that I noticed the first quadrant of their map had been produced upside down and backwards. This map had been generated for national distribution, yet had a major error that nobody caught before it was printed and distributed. During this same year, my Missinaibi guidebook was released, correcting all topographic information. In the last fourteen years there have been no canoe-related deaths along the river, chiefly because the Ontario government finally took the initiative to erect proper signage, and supported a concise guidebook that made sure the public was informed.

Canada is a nation of wild rivers. The Missinaibi took the lives of thirty-four people over a seventeen-year period. Over the past three decades there may have been hundreds of deaths across Canada attributed to faulty maps and lack of "duty of care" by parks and provincial government administrations. These same bureaucracies have spent millions of tax dollars on advertising wild Canada and eco-adventure recreation, but almost nothing on accurate, field-truthed support material. Adventurers love to scan maps, longing to find precipitous gradient drops and wild rapids ... it's part of our addiction to rivers and wilderness. Selling maps is big business for EMR, peddling more than 630,000 maps each year. But even if the adventuring public is provided with the best information possible, there exists those who cannot "read" maps or interpret the information from a map to actual landscape visuals. In addition, there are those who put too much faith in topographic maps; in many instances the wilderness traveller relaxes into the gear threshold instead of learning the required hard skills. International adventurers coming to this country for a wilderness experience rely on the information provided, and trust that government tourism agencies have done their field work ... in the least, provide the same calibre of maps that they can purchase in their own country. When they get here they are presented with a topographic chart produced half a century ago, maps intended for political reasons, to designate ownership, for military use and resource extraction ... not for recreational travel along a wilderness trail.

EIGHT
GETTING LOST

We're not lost. We're locationally challenged.
— John M. Ford

I have to work hard to get turned around in the bush, or disoriented, and I've been in that situation on a few occasions, but I've never actually been lost. There have been times when I wasn't quite sure of my exact location, usually while travelling in the Far North where the topography is often dead level. I once sailed down the coast of Hudson Bay in two canoes tied together, at night, with the use of a compass only; granted, full darkness was brief, but during that time the only indication of my location in relation to the shore was in the rocks I would run into while the tide was going out. It was unnerving, especially since polar bears like to hide behind boulders, and it was almost a relief to bounce off the odd rock with the assurance that the shore was less than a kilometre away. But there were moments of mild panic when at times we seemed to be straying off the course with no sight references to go by. Others had perished on the Bay doing what we were doing — the inimical coast and its deadly winds are unforgiving.

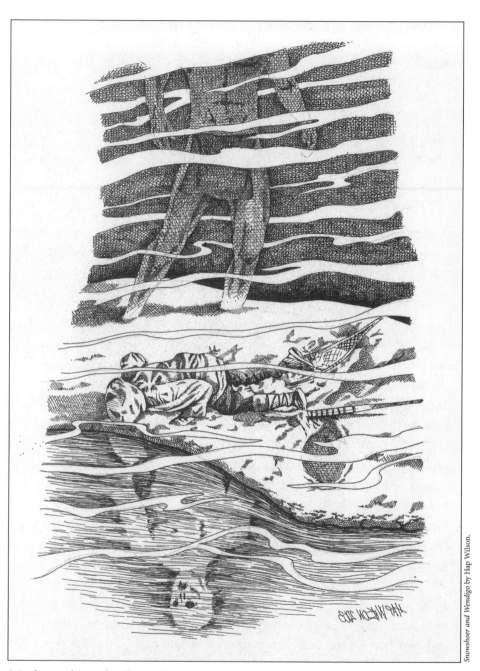

Wendigo is alive and well ... and waiting.

Search Ends for Hiker Lost in B.C. Woods, September 3, 2008, CBC News

[The]RCMP has called off a search for a German hiker who vanished 40 days ago in the wilderness of northern B.C.

Boats, planes and helicopters scoured the area, and searchers did find evidence of his journey. His backpack was found on a sandbar in the Kechika River upstream from Terminus Mountain. A pouch containing his passport, map, and papers was found in a logjam on the Gataga River. "We're assuming something happened to him and he lost his life," RCMP Staff Sgt. Tom Roy said. "He either fell in the river or befell some other misfortune."

The German hiker may not have been lost, but when you don't show up at the appropriate time for a pickup, the red flag goes up. The authorities deem this person "missing" or lost. Solo adventurers assume one of the greatest risks while travelling in the wilderness. By travelling alone there is no other person available to come to the rescue should something go awry. Most people get lost while on their own. If a trail is not well-marked, either by footpath or by sign, it's not difficult to lose your way if you don't pay attention. Birdwatchers are particularly susceptible to straying off the path, getting lured deeper into the bush while trying to identify a species or peering too long through binoculars or camera lens. Hunters also fall victim to their own inexperience at orienteering and survival. Every year, hundreds of North Americans get lost, injured, or even die while hiking through remote sections of national or provincial parks and other wild areas. These incidents, all of them, are preventable.

Before the advent of cellphones, emergency locating beacons, global positioning systems, and satellite phones, travelling in the bush demanded more attention to detail and direction. Technology, again, with the availability of instant communication and wayfinding, has eliminated the need for basic orienteering skills — the reading of "sign" is no longer required. For today's adventurer, the dependency on such gear is paramount, and like all the other outdoor clothing and accouterment, an outdoor enthusiast is judged by the quality and extent of his kit. It is now typical to find people in the outdoors fully loaded down with the latest and most expensive gear, but still lacking in woods etiquette and trail skills.

At the last rapid on the Seal River in northern Manitoba, Deaf Rapids — a rather vicious maelstrom of turbulent river dropping fifty vertical feet into ocean tidewater — I was forced to sit upstream with my group, waiting three hours for the tide to come in before attempting to run the rapids. Locating this particular nasty piece of whitewater is sometimes difficult because of the fog that rolls in from Hudson Bay and the endless approach rapids that lead up to it. And because of the abrupt pitch off into the ocean, there is no visible or even audible warning that the rapid is near. In a case such as this, the only tactical procedure is to follow the topographical map with birds-eye precision, counting down every turn or twist in the river, noting each braid as the river fans out in multiple channels, at the same time taking sight references as you manoeuvre through the whitewater. It's not easy to keep looking at a map while running difficult whitewater in a canoe … but it's absolutely necessary.

We ran Deaf Rapids at eleven o'clock at night, when the tide was full and it was still light enough to navigate up the coast to the sanctity of a goose-hunt shack (safe from polar bears). The next day, at low tide, another canoe group arrived. They were in a sorry state, having dumped in the rapids with near-death circumstances. The leader, as it turned out, had no maps at all but was relying on his GPS for directional prompting. Unable to determine exactly where he was, he had inadvertently led his group into the vortex of Deaf Rapids where they all capsized. Even armed with the most expensive global positioning system, the guide was lost, albeit momentarily, but enough to put his group in peril.

The inherent problem, and the primary reason people get lost or turned around, even when armed with topographic maps and GPS, lies in the fact that they have trouble interpreting information on a map. For some, it's a distance/time enigma — judging how far you've travelled in a specific amount of time — for others, it's a direct interpretation perplexity — computing real, three-dimensional landscapes onto a two-dimensional map. The accuracy of the GPS is astounding, but you are still expected to have a certain comprehension of eye-visual-to-map understanding. And like all outdoor skills, map reading comes with experience.

Canoeists get lost constantly while portaging their gear. It happened to me, years ago, but it's frightening how easily it can happen. And in the Canadian wilderness there is no such thing as a shortcut; trying to locate an easier, shorter way to arrive at a destination usually besets a world of trouble. Canoeists today are notorious for trying to find an easier or quicker way around obstacles because of their latent distaste for portaging.

On my first canoe trip to Temagami in 1970, I was solo paddling with the accompaniment of a couple of friends. We ventured up the torturous portages of the north channel of the Lady Evelyn River and had decided to portage (bushwhack) cross-country to the south branch of the river instead of continuing upstream to the lake that divides the two. My friends went off with their packs, which was the wiser thing to do, but I had decided to carry my canoe over unfamiliar ground where there was no trail. The stretch on the map showed a shortcut of about four hundred metres, but after trudging twice that distance through a mélange of deadfall, rock, and impenetrable tag alder, I eventually heard the sound of running water. Thinking I was near the other channel, I pushed on; but when I reached the shore of the river, I was perplexed as to how I managed to get to the opposite side of the rapids *and* why the current was flowing in the wrong direction. I put down my canoe. About fifty feet away I noticed a pack sitting by the shore. It was mine. I had gone full circle and returned almost precisely to the spot where I started portaging! Embarrassed and not wanting my friends to know of my error, I grabbed my pack and ran to catch up with them.

This kind of directional miscarriage is not always reserved for the individual. I've seen whole groups get lost while portaging across a prospective shortcut. One of my regular customers while I was in the outfitting business was the Queen's Fifth Regiment from England. This elite group of soldiers, about twenty crack militiamen, was to go on a "work" vacation — a wilderness canoe trip in Canada. I outfitted them and designed a route that would challenge their abilities. One week into their trip, they decided to make a shortcut over a swath of land that would cut short their trip by about five kilometres. The distance would be about one kilometre overland. Carrying their gear from Point A to Point B seemed to be a simple matter. Half carried packs while the others shouldered canoes, and off they went in more than one direction. After wandering for about an hour, the soldiers who were still more or less banded together dropped their gear midway across the shortcut and tried desperately to find their way back to the start point. After some time they located the remainder of their gear along with a few confounded compatriots, loaded up and trekked off in what they thought was the direction of their selected target. Another hour had lapsed but they arrived, with some difficulty, at the lake where they were supposed to be. But there was no sign of the others. Striking off in the direction of where they thought they left their first load, they got thoroughly confused and ended up back in the same place. After much shouting, the men finally began to assemble on the far shore but without most of their packs and tents which had been left somewhere midway along the shortcut. They spent a rainy night without their tents and a good deal of their personal gear, huddled under canoes at the end of their shortcut. They retrieved their lost gear the next morning. The one hour it would have originally taken to remain on their original route, took almost an entire additional day to sort out the mess they created by attempting a shorter route.

NINE
ANIMAL ATTACK

Wild animals never kill for sport. Man is the only one to whom the torture and death of his fellow creatures is amusing in itself.
— James A. Froude (1818–1894)

I worry about Tony. He's a big man and shows absolutely no fear in the presence of large predators, or for that matter, any animal either above him on the food chain, or physically larger than he is. Tony Grant manages the Aspen Valley Wildlife Sanctuary in Muskoka, Ontario, a quarter of a kilometre down the road from where I live. Tony is the only one who works there that can get in the cage with the captive lioness and play with her. Sometimes she lies on top of Tony and won't let him get up for half an hour. He hand-feeds her raw chicken and she pines when Tony is away. She could kill Tony in a flash of nail and claw anytime she felt like it. I worry about Tony because animal trainers and handlers get killed often enough, eventually, and it's simply the immutable law of the wild. I look at animal handlers as I do mountain climbers and other extreme adventurers who live on the edge and sometimes push the limits — they invariably forget about those laws. And you only have to lift your guard once. So, I worry about Tony because he's a good neighbour.

I live in Muskoka, or cottage country, known for its million-dollar

Coyote Head by Hap Wilson.

What do we really know about Nature?

summer homes, voguish shops, executive golf courses, and fractional ownership developments. Strangely enough, I've seen more wildlife out my back window at home, and had more close-up confrontations with wild animals than in any of my far-flung travels across the Canadian northland. I live on the fringe of settlement; it's a congenial mix of forested and open land, perfect for coyote, wolf, moose, deer, bear, or any wild species you would normally find ranging around more northerly regions of the province. I can look out my window and watch deer grazing in the field, moose rutting in October, or have black bears ravaging through my compost box in the backyard. Last month two black bears killed all my chickens. I had to dispatch one of the more aggressive male bears because it was unpredictable, testy, and a threat to my children who play in the woods adjacent to the house (and compost box). And I don't want to get rid of my compost box. My daughter's lunch bag and schoolwork pack was hauled out of the back of my pickup truck by a bear. And bears are known to drag off rather large items, including dogs, kids, and full garbage containers. The teacher reprimanded my daughter for making up the story and not doing her homework; it wasn't until we sent a picture of the bear to the school, standing on top of our kitchen stove in the house, that my daughter found any closure in the matter.

Any wild animal is unpredictable; and we think we know more than we do about Nature, thanks to Disney and the world of anthropomorphized animated characters. A caged animal in a sanctuary that may have shown only the friendliest attitude toward humans may have some rogue primitive spark in their cerebrum that initiates an unprovoked attack. Or maybe it was just having a bad day. The case of the young handler who climbed into the wolf enclosure at the Haliburton wildlife sanctuary, unsupervised, thinking that the pack alpha female wouldn't mind at all, was one of tragic misconception. As a result, she suffered a horrible death ... and all the wolves were shot by local police in retaliation.

My brother was a cop for York Regional police back in the early 1980s. He was called to a country property, the home of a renowned bear trainer, where a woman had just been killed by a "pet" black bear. The trainer was in the habit of letting the bear out of its compound so the cage could be cleaned. The man's girlfriend was asleep in the bedroom when the bear entered and started to maul her. She attempted to climb out the window but the bear clawed her legs so viciously, trying to drag her back in to the house that she bled to death in a matter of a few minutes. When the bear was finished, her legs looked as if they had been put through a shredding machine. It was surmised that the bear was attracted by the scent of a woman who was on her menstrual cycle. In fact, some parks agencies will not allow woman employees to go out into wild bear country during their period.

The fact that animals are more dangerous when they live in proximity to humans is not a surprise. More people obviously mean more incidents. Animals can display unusual characteristics, lose their normal fear of people, and people sometimes lose their sensibilities while experiencing an animal "event." Heavily used parks are a good example. On a road trip through Yellowstone Park in Wyoming some years ago, there were several cars pulled over and a man was feeding a mother black bear through the window of his camper. Meanwhile, another man ran at the two cubs that accompanied the mother, attempting to snap a few pictures. The cubs bolted, crying in fear with the cameraman in hot pursuit. When the mother bear heard the cries of her two cubs she forgot about the handout and ran at the man with the camera, moving at almost twice the speed of the running man. Luckily, the man diverted an attack by climbing on top of a nearby car.

In Algonquin Provincial Park, where most animals, both large and small, have been subject to all manner of studies and surveys, one can view moose at any time of the day along the Highway 60 corridor that runs through the park. Again, with cars stopped on both sides of the road, a man was trying to photograph a moose calf while its mother, nearby, hackles raised on the back of her neck, paced nervously back and forth. Little did the man with the camera realize that a cow moose is a deadly threat. Take for example the case a few years ago in Alaska where a man was kicked to death by a cow moose protecting her calf — right in front of a public building, captured on film by an onlooker.

In March of 2005, a cow moose came into the yard and began licking the road salt off my truck that was parked in the driveway. I went outside to chase her off when she began tugging at the wiper blades with her teeth. I soon realized that it wasn't interested in going anywhere. I did a little human-animal bonding test by inserting rice crackers I keep in the glovebox for my kids, into the side of the moose's mouth. And that's an interesting bit of moose trivia if you ever get the opportunity to hand-feed a moose; because of the size of their snout, they can't take snacks from your palm like a horse. Moose have this strange lip thing going on, raised at the side in a kind of sardonic grin — a perfect place to shove rice crackers. She then followed me around the truck, nudging my shoulder for more crackers. I scratched her behind the ears and combed my fingers through her neck hair. I went back in the house, got my two young children, and placed them in the box of the truck so they could watch from a safe perch. When the cow nudged up beside my kids they were allowed to put their arms around its neck. I took a picture.

Now, when I look back at this episode, I think that even if this cow had been released from a wildlife sanctuary, it was a stupid thing for me to do. I rely on my instinct, maybe too much so; even though I had a generally good feeling about this cow moose and the somewhat secure location of my kids, I didn't allow for the remote possibility that this cow moose might be a bit mercurial in nature. It did make for some interesting family photographs though.

Everybody has an animal tale they like to tell, and when a bunch of casual adventurers get together there's always a vigorous competition about who has the best or most outrageous wild animal story. I'll usually relax into the banter, listening to chronicles about chipmunks in the peanut butter jar, and the saga with the mouse building a nest in the bottom of the food pack, a couple of moose sightings and maybe a bear sniffing around a campsite. Then, when the stories thin out, it's my call to step in.

Call it swagger, call it braggadocio, but I love telling this story because it's so bizarre. And few people believe it when I tell them, anyway, so I'm more likely to be branded a liar than a braggart. Two years ago I received a frenzied phone call from my other neighbour down the road, claiming that a bull moose was rampaging in her backyard and attacking her husband's tarped boat. Pat was alone in the house and had just enough time to place two calls — one to me and one to Tony at the sanctuary — before the moose tore up a trough of sod on the lawn and cut off the phone line! I drove my pickup truck to her house thinking this would be an easy task to carry out. I'd corral and drive the bull using my truck and force it down their back lane onto an open field near the Rosseau River and that would be the end of it. When I arrived, the bull had its antlers under the plastic boat tarp and was tugging at it as if sparring with another bull. It was literally dragging a one-ton trailered boat across the lawn. I pulled my truck in behind it and laid on the horn. The moose retreated from its fight with the boat and I was able to "herd" it down the laneway and out in to the field, exactly as planned. *That was easy,* I thought, but the natural world always has its peculiarities that challenge what you may think or believe to be true: Don't believe everything you think.

On my way back up the laneway to the house, feeling good about my quick success, I saw the bull's head reflected in my rearview mirror. *It was actually trying to pass me!* I parked my truck in Pat's parking lot, got out, and stood with my back against the side of the garage by the back lawn. The moose now made wide circles on the lawn in front of me, trotting slowly, keeping an eye on my movements. Pat was standing near the backdoor of the house when Tony finally arrived and sized up the situation. It was October, rutting season, and bull moose have been known to attack oncoming trains and roll over the occasional car. Tony and I looked at each other and smiled nervously. *Now what?* Tony said that he'd just finished feeding the captive cow moose at the sanctuary and that he probably had her smell all over him. I certainly didn't notice but the bull did. He abruptly stopped his circling, waved his head from side to side, drooled and grunted, then approached Tony with his head lowered to the ground. Tony remained motionless. The bull then sniffed Tony from head to foot, turned and looked at me, head still lowered, eyes red and glowering, and the hackles rising on the back of his neck. *Shit, this doesn't look good.*

I have had enough contact with wild animals to know not to make eye contact. I quickly diverted my eyes but watched the bull's movements closely and hoped it wouldn't charge. I was wrong. With head still lowered it moved toward me, not at a run but it closed the distance between us in seconds. I also knew enough not to run. I kept my eyes glued on the bull's antlers and the sharp multi-pointed spears of bone heading directly for my abdomen. I dug my feet into the turf and grabbed at the moose's antlers. I had no other choice. The next few moments were terrifying, not knowing what was going to happen; I could be dead on my neighbour's lawn in five minutes. Pat thought Tony and I were both going to be killed.

But the moose just toyed with me, tugging gently, lightly jerking with me while I held on, trying to keep the antlers from ramming into my belly. At least by holding on I could keep the points at a safe distance; but if he wanted to, he could propel me through the side of the garage. Instead, we sparred gently but the jerks were getting more aggressive. "Tony, I don't like this situation," I remember saying through pursed lips.

"I'll try something," Tony assured, and began walking down the laneway toward the river. It was brilliant. The bull pulled away and started to follow Tony down the hill, so close, in fact, that his head was touching Tony's shoulder. I assured Tony that I would follow from a safe distance and watch, just in case the bull turned on him. But it didn't; the moose followed Tony across the field, along the river, and through a marsh that led to the sanctuary almost a kilometre away. By the time I got back in my truck and drove down the road to the sanctuary, Tony had led the bull moose into the compound that held the cow.

This was not unusual characteristics displayed by a somewhat quasi-domesticated moose with a seasonal hormonal imbalance; I can testify with authority that the lure of female company can make men stupid. Tony assured me that this particular bull had not been a sanctuary moose. As for his behaviour, he was doing what comes naturally, based on instinct and olfactory sensations, not to say much for his choice of female companionship. Tony did have the right aroma, and I had stationed myself as the competition for Tony. Regardless of the comic intonations of the situation, it remained entirely unpredictable while it was unfolding. Personally, I try not to get into this type of close confrontation, but as a wilderness guide and wildlife photographer I find that these encounters happen frequently enough.

It's one thing to be looking for large animals to photograph or study, it's quite another affair when they either seek you out, or you come in contact by sheer chance and circumstance. Seeking out wildlife by design requires a stout knowledge of animal behaviour; you control the situation so long as you don't push your luck. A couple of years back I was hiking the tundra in the Thelon River headwater area, about eight kilometres west of Whitefish Lake in the Northwest Territories. It was open country, defined by sand eskers, small kettle lakes, felsenmeer (broken rock), and willow scrub.

Tundra wolves were a common sight, but I was looking specifically for muskoxen. I climbed a high ridge for a better view beyond and came upon a herd of oxen — four calves and twelve adults, grazing on the flats across a pond at the base of the hill. The wind was in my favour and, so long as I kept the pond between me and them, I could get quite close to the herd. Approaching them as if I were just another muskox, bent over and pausing every few moments to "graze," I was able to get within fifty metres to snap the shots I wanted. The bulls had formed a circle around the females and the young muskoxen. When I approached a bit too close, two bulls broke away from the circle and made a wide swing to come in behind me. I retreated slowly. The one bull was now downwind of where I stood and caught my scent; in an instant the whole herd was on the move.

Muskoxen can be dangerous at close range and they have been known to gore people to death with their horns. Normally, oxen are seen ambling along the shores of northern rivers and lakes and confrontations are unlikely. One of my clients, however, while paddling the Coppermine River, had an unforgettable experience with a muskox while fishing. We were camped at a rapid, still within the treed zone of the river, and Norm went off downstream to fish for trout. Lake trout were visible at the surface along the shore and it was no problem to catch one. After latching on to an exceptionally large trout, Norm had to walk along the shore in an attempt to keep it on the light line he was using. While doing so, he almost tripped over a muskox that was lying on the turf beside the river. The animal was not at all pleased at being disturbed but Norm refused to let go of his rod with the trophy lake trout that was to be our dinner still attached. Norm and the muskox backed away from each other and retreated safely; the trout ended up in the fry pan for dinner.

This was a case of sudden and unexpected encounter, and in almost all instances, regardless of species, the abruptness of contact sends both parties scurrying for safe cover. This has happened to me on a number of occasions, with wolf, moose, and bear, and each time the animal has bolted. It's not good practice to run from a bear, but to back away slowly without making eye contact. Three situations can be of concern: getting in between the mother and its young (primarily moose and bear); paddling a canoe directly in front of a swimming animal; and disturbing a bear's fresh kill site.

My own research into fatal or near-fatal animal attacks puts humans as the cause of the confrontation: hiking in restricted zones where bear have been sighted and noted as a risk; getting too close for photographic opportunities; despoiling the campsite with garbage or fish cleaning; ignorance of wildlife habits and their respective environments.

While camping in polar bear country, usually along the Hudson Bay coastline, I always employ a "watch" system through the Arctic night, each camper taking a one to two-hour watch. Polar bear have been known to stalk humans, and now with the shortage of food offshore and the effects of global warming, these predators range several hundred kilometres inland. This alters the dynamic of Arctic travel and the level of caution employed. Modern voyageurs are well-equipped with hard gear but often naive about wildlife and their habits, failing to learn enough about potential problems so that when something does happen, they are ill-prepared. Some wilderness guides scoff at the idea of bringing a rifle along during trips in grizzly or polar bear country, and have never had a confrontation. Others who carry guns regularly seem to have more incidents of wildlife "events" simply, perhaps, because of the questionable gun karma. I stopped taking a gun along on my trips because of the weight and general nuisance trying to keep it from rusting. Instead, I carry a bear-blaster pen that lobs power-packed firecrackers about seventy-five metres, hopefully in front of a nosy bear and not behind it. It takes a couple of shots to get the distance down to an art — one displaced shot could turn the bear at a fast sprint toward you.

My late friend Bob Hunter, co-founder of Greenpeace, of whom I had the pleasure of sharing a canoe with on many a wayward adventure, was deathly afraid of bears. On a trip down the Caribou River in northern Manitoba, near the Nunavut border, we came into contact with a polar bear near the Hudson Bay coast. Our group was enjoying a quiet shore lunch when a bear approached across the river and ambled down to the shore. Everyone grabbed their cameras and took pictures. When the bear slid silently into the river, no more than seventy-five metres away, and started to swim toward us, the cameras were quickly dispensed and everyone turned to me — the guide — wondering what I was going to do to protect them. I had a twelve-gauge shotgun with me with two magazines

— one with bear-blasters, and the other with hollow-nose slugs. The last thing I wanted to do was to shoot a bear. Knowing that a polar bear is a proficient swimmer, I quickly peeled the gun from its case and loaded the clip with the blasters. Before I could fire a warning shot, the bear seemed to sense something and abruptly turned back toward shore where it quickly disappeared over the boulder field downriver. Since we were heading in that direction not knowing exactly where the bear would be, fear and trepidation prevailed until we cleared the area and had paddled a good five kilometres downstream. Bob was now paranoid about bear confrontations and insisted on setting his tent up close to mine because I had the gun. Bob was a dear soul to me, and he had some residual habits carried over from the Greenpeace days — he liked his bit of weed and a mickey of rye before he crashed for the night; he would practice drawing his knife from its sheath (not to stab the bear but to cut a retreat hole in the back of the tent), test to see how fast he could take the safety off the can of bear spray (much to the chagrin of his tent-mates), and finally lining his knife, bear spray, and whistle alongside his sleeping bag. Bob would pop a couple of sleeping pills, slip on his eye mask, and then fall asleep literally dead to the world. I told Bob that he wouldn't have to worry because the bear would probably think he was dead, anyway, and move on.

I had a black bear step over me as I slept in the open on a beach in Algonquin Park. He was on his way to the food pack which was leaning up against a tree nearby. I was sixteen at the time and I was terrified. Three boys had been mauled to death by a black bear earlier that season on the Petawawa River. They had been fishing and had wiped the fish smell on their clothing. My friends and I peered cautiously out of our sleeping bags as the bear wrestled with our pack. We had been windbound for two days and had run out of food so the bear quickly lost interest in the empty pack and wandered off. Since then I have had no less than a hundred bear encounters, mostly while homesteading north of Mattawa, Ontario, — a community renowned for its bear poaching prowess.

Every bear has its own personality, much like humans do, and that's why the bear was revered by people of the First Nations as a sacred being. Skinned out, a bear looks just like a human, except for the skull and claws. It's also smart. A bear can quickly figure out how to get a suspended pack down from a tree hoist (bear piñata), or set off a leg trap by dragging brush over it … or tear open the side of a tent to get at the package of trail mix buried in the side pocket of a day pack. Bears are moody creatures, and if they find food at someone's campsite they are reluctant to leave it; and they'll keep coming back no matter how many pots you bang, air horns you blast, or sticks you throw at it. The only recourse is to move to another

Black Bear by Ingrid Zschogner.

Makwa — sacred bear — just doing her job.

site. It's actually not hard to tell if a bear has been frequenting a campsite. Campers could save themselves a lot of grief if they were to first scan the general area looking for bear scat. If previous campers left garbage, fish entrails and even human feces scattered about, then it's best to move on. Overturned rocks and logs signature a bears search for grubs, hornets, and ants — what they'll eat between visits by campers.

I've spent a lot of time on the trail and for the number of kilometres travelled, have had few threats from wildlife; but then I'm careful to avoid such circumstances … most of the time. I've had more grief from smaller animals such as cabin mice who think nothing of nibbling at your knuckle joint or earlobe as you sleep. I've had snowshoe hare pounce on top of my sleeping bag and pummel me with their legs while I slept out on the rocks by the lake edge, and female ruffed grouse smack into my head on a trail when I got too close to her young. These are not exactly death fearing encounters but are the norm for most trips in the wild. I have to say that the more I learned about the nature of wild animals, the fewer confrontations I had and the greater the number of positive experiences that keep things in the right perspective.

Canoe Paddling with Skeletons by Hap Wilson.

The fool is never alone in the wilderness.

TEN
INEPTITUDE

Only two things are infinite, the universe and human stupidity,
and I'm not sure about the former.
— Albert Einstein (1879–1955)

Years ago I was privy to an experience that changed the way I looked at human intellect under certain extreme conditions. There was a grass fire raging near some country homes located just off the southern rim of the Oak Ridges Moraine, and it had yet to be contained by the firefighters. We were watching nervously from my friends' house as the fire swept up close to a neighbour's yard where a team of firefighters tried to hold the front line but were having difficulty. A woman suddenly ran from the house clutching her baby to her chest, screaming hysterically, and headed directly toward the oncoming inferno. Only metres from the encroaching flames, she had to be tackled by one of the firefighters and pulled to safety.

My thoughts on how people deal with panic situations has been manifested through years of wilderness travel and related research. Canadian history books are resonant with stories of human stupidity, particularly when speaking of wilderness travel and survival. The first Europeans to set foot on Canadian soil were shamefully negligent at surviving, and too stubborn to seek the wisdom of the aboriginal inhabitants. Centuries later, reports of deaths in remote places still surface, often, and their causes born from stupidity and ignorance.

Not long ago, four young paddlers finish a paddling trip down the Albany River in northern Ontario. Not a difficult or technical river, the Albany terminates at the Cree village of Fort Albany on the coast of James Bay. From there, canoeists normally fly the short distance south to Moosonee where they can then take the polar bear express train back to their point of departure. It's not that expensive a flight. Instead, the paddlers decide to sail the two hundred kilometres down the coast in order to save money on flight costs. Believing that if they tied their two canoes together they would create a more seaworthy craft, it wouldn't be a problem. Safety wouldn't be an issue. Fort Albany locals tried to dissuade them, even offering to boat them down to Moosonee in a motor launch. It was a stretch of coastline that was incessantly hammered by north winds with little shelter along the way. Deaths and disappearances were common enough along the James Bay coast. They set off from the village headed for Moosonee even though the weather was turning to the worse. Two boys and two girls, all in their early twenties, never showed up in Moosonee, and their bodies were never discovered. Life jackets and other remnants of this mishap were discovered scattered along the beaches some time later. What it must have been like for these young paddlers, as their craft faltered and broke apart in heavy seas, and the ice-cold water, must have been horrific.

Self-assuming decisions, like this one made by inexperienced paddlers, cost them their lives and forever affected the lives of their families. In the outdoors, in the wilderness, crass and thick-headed decisions are often made with a particular zeal reserved only for vainglorious attempts to defy Nature. It's far easier to make a stupid decision than to think things out, to strategize, or to weigh the consequences; but the question arises, most assuredly, *why in the wilderness is it so easy to construct your own death?* Assumptions prevail, but it may rest on the fact that we often transport our city-evolved complacency with us when we walk the backwoods trail. Racing down the freeway at 120 kilometres per hour, weaving in and out of traffic in a tiny bubble of metal, cellphone or coffee cup in the free hand, is something we all do mindlessly and without fear. We worry more about getting caught speeding than the circumstance of a possible crash. We are inviolable. Armed with the same mindset, adventurers will descend upon the wilderness with a protracted cognizance of their own safety. I've often heard debutant whitewater paddlers exclaim to me, "how hard can it be!" and with absolutely no training, push off down a rapid with frightening faith — a dogma that almost always terminates in disaster, sooner or later. This particular adherence to passive self-destruction is rampant. Today, along the wilderness path there are no stupid decisions ... all actions are commandeered under the auspices of "adventure spirit," primed and manifested by television shows that epitomize life in the wilderness through extreme survival programming. This form of entertainment does nothing to prepare us for the realities of trail life, true adventure or, most importantly, the necessary smarts to stay alive. The actors engaged in bringing us this form of perverted amusement well know that they will be rescued (getting voted off without usurping the money prize is the worst that could happen). Most television survival-themed shows rely on creating stunts that are simply theatrical acts of stupidity. And because of our insatiable hunger for this type of entertainment pleasure, it is the very reason why we take this form of evolved survival mentality with us to the woods. We forget to think. In the wilderness the only safety rope is the one you knot or cinch yourself, and there is no lunch wagon parked behind the film set.

Then there is the stigma attached to those who may be incompetent, or novice, or inexperienced and won't admit that they *just don't have the skills*. And this is problematic for the guide, the instructor, the leader, or for general group dynamics. Particularly for outdoor travel in the wilderness, techniques have changed, and the quality of outdoor gear has improved. Post-Boomers who spent one or more memorable summers at a canoe camp when they were kids, now want to descend on that same wilderness loaded down with kids, a catatonic wife, and forty extra pounds around the midriff. What seemed to be an uncomplicated family adventure often turns out to be a disaster.

The twenty or so years that have lapsed between youthful camp days and the present weren't likely spent on the trail honing outdoor skills. When Dad tries to recreate the good old days and suddenly realizes he doesn't quite know what to do to facilitate the basic needs of his family, the adventure quickly turns sour. And it doesn't take much to create dissent amongst the ranks.

The axiom that implies that all food cooked in the great outdoors tastes better is a gross misnomer. It's easy to kill bannock bread fried over a fire that's too hot, and the beans and rice you had as a kid camper just doesn't appease the appetites of picky kids, and instant coffee isn't the same as the roastery blend mom buys at the market. If dad doesn't cook at home, and suddenly becomes the bon vivant of the backwoods, then trouble is brewing in the stewpot. Then there's the thing with the tent that leaks because it's sitting in a depression that fills with rain ... and the bugs!

Family camping is wonderful, and kids are malleable when it comes to adapting to new environments, so long as all their basic needs are met. Knowing what gear to take along and packing for rainy days builds a strong foundation for success, but I've seen too many Type-A achiever dads bull ahead into the unknown, family in tow, trying to recreate something that appeared to be simple during their camp days.

Good camping and wilderness travel skills take time to perfect, at least to the point that transcends raw survival tactics employed by the unpracticed. There are so many tricks to this trade that make life so much easier and enjoyable; the secret is in the planning and prevention. In the survival mode, all basic elements that are required to sustain life could be compromised, one by one, and very quickly depending on the situation. This may happen when a canoe capsizes and gear is lost, or soaked through because it wasn't waterproofed and secured. It could be raining, windy, cool or worse, and everything is sodden — even the spare change of clothes and you can't get a fire going. Tents may not be secured or pitched taught; that sag in the rain fly is enough to pool the water where you don't want it. No axe or saw? After three or four days of cold rain in September you'd wished you had brought them along. But even if you did, you may not have known how to get dry wood, anyway.

I've passed many people on the trail in various stages of wretchedness, and their misery was most often the result of poor leadership and planning: forgotten equipment, trip was too hard, no protection from biting insects, lousy food, wet and cold — all things that are generally the responsibility of the trip leader to know how to remedy. But, in most cases, the appointed chief never admitted his shortcomings, whether too embarrassed, stubborn or indifferent. *How hard can wilderness trekking be?* Well, it can be very hard.

When I took my wilderness first aid course it was at a well-known canoe and kayak school. I was there for eight days. They call it a canoe school but their techniques are predominantly aggressive whitewater kayak that they've cross-pollinated with canoe techniques. On the last day of my course the school had bussed in a load of fresh kayak students, mostly older high-school kids, full of beans and high expectations. The first thing the school did was to perch them in front of a theatre screen to watch a film showing kayakers vaulting their boats off cliffs and waterfalls.

Now you have to ask yourself, first of all, unless you were vying for the universal Darwin Award, why you would want to kayak over a waterfall? But you could see such delight on the faces of these inner-city kids, watching as kayak after kayak plummeted over steeper and gnarlier precipices, shouts of "Right on!" and "Totally, dude!" resounding in the auditorium. Extreme films showing extreme stunts are slick marketing tactics of the gear companies, again, steering trends toward a particular mindset. And there are more people buying kayaks than canoes today, for two reasons: the younger crowd aspires to paddle over waterfalls and dangerous rapids (canoes are no longer sexy); while the more conservative market purchase the "sit-on-top" and sea-kayak because it takes little skill to get the boat to go where you want it. For most novices it is difficult to learn how to solo paddle a canoe and stay in control, especially in the wind; but with a kayak there's no need for a "correction" stroke and you're already placed in the appropriate position just behind midpoint. The first inclination of a would-be solo paddler is to sit in the stern seat, at the very back of the canoe where one would normally steer the boat from if there were two people paddling. This causes the bow, or front, to rise out of the water, which acts like a wind sail, destabilizing the canoe, causing the occupant to be blown down the lake, no matter how hard they try to fight against the wind. Yet again we find ourselves fighting against Nature instead of adapting to it.

Whitewater canoeing down rapids is a white, European phenomenon brought to this country by the likes of the Hudson's Bay Company. Time was money; and to get men, equipment, and trade items into the frontier, and furs back out in a timely fashion, river rapids were often run with loaded canoes because it was far quicker than carrying supplies over the portage trails. Native Canadians watched the white traders in horror, beguiled by the insanity of such stupidity and lack of reverence for the power of the river. People of the First Nations were not driven by greed or time constraints and treated their bark canoes as the frail things they actually were. And along some of the historic trade routes, like the French River in Ontario, treasure hunting divers have located a surfeit of antique guns and trade items at the bottom of rapids.

But I get caught up in the water play, too; it's dangerous fun, but less risky if you actually know what you're doing and keep within the boundary of your experience. Unfortunately, many fledgling adventurers want to skip the formality of learning the basics, and jump right in to the more aggressive or "exotic" exploits. These people have money. And they buy their way to the summit of Everest even if they have to be short-roped by a Sherpa guide and literally carried to the top. The professional super-achiever type mainstreamers tend to sway toward the immediacy of return benefits from extreme adventure.

Once revered as a male-dominated sport, whitewater canoeing has attained a more balanced gender definition. And in my business I've noticed that not just men have raging egos and rampant testosterone. This was evident one summer when I booked four women on a private whitewater trip down the Temagami River. They were friends, all from the same legal firm in Toronto, and had taken up whitewater canoeing just the year before. They went to a couple of weekend clinics (actually the same kayak school mentioned earlier) where they learned aggressive techniques. The Temagami River is an intermediate class whitewater river and it would be the women's first river trip.

They arrived at my outfitting store in two BMW's (one would have sufficed), dressed in expensive outerwear, money practically oozing out of their pockets. I was to be their guide and instructor. They looked me up and down, glanced at the beater-canoes with the rippled hulls and cross-hatched gouges, a look of total disdain on their collective faces, and asked if "this was a joke?" I explained that I hadn't yet succumbed to the outdoor garment industry consumerism (I still bought my army fatigues at surplus stores and wore a thirty-dollar rain jacket), and that my canoes were beaters because I wouldn't take a good Kevlar canoe down a bony river with novice paddlers.

"We're not novice," commanded the group of well-dressed women. And I was eyed with suspicion. *"We have our certificates!"* Politely I explained that a weekend clinic running the same rapid over and over again, and having lunch in a cafeteria, was not quite the same as plunging down an entire river system, fully loaded with all your camping gear.

We began the river trip at an adjoining lake which I preferred because I like to see if a paddler has basic flatwater skills and steering strokes first before getting into any fast water. I'm a firm believer in starting at the most basic of skills and working up to aggressive water play once you've mastered the primary strokes. The four women were in two canoes while I solo paddled mine. I wasn't at all surprised to see the two canoes zigzagging down the lake, out of control in the light wind. They had no idea how to steer their canoes in a straight line. And when I tried to correct them, they were impatient and testy, telling me that they came for the whitewater and not the open lakes. I was firm and explained that I wasn't taking them anywhere unless they learned how to control their boats; and I told them this because I know that you cannot work the rapids if you don't feel the nuances of your canoe on flat water first. Whitewater paddling is somewhat like dancing with a good partner — it's disastrous if you're out of sync with each other; but if you can communicate through motion and finesse, there's a lovely symbiosis and fluidity of movement.

Aside from the few whitewater strokes they had learned at the clinic, they knew virtually nothing about canoeing, and had no interest in the trip as an enlightening journey. I knew they had preconceived notions of exercising their new-found talents and were on a high at the onset of the trip. But I dashed their spirit with a heavy dose of reality, and they did realize that their ignorance of the demanded skills could have cost them had they struck out on their own. It wasn't a good trip for any of us; they felt a bit overzealous and embarrassed, and I had to crush their hubris for their own good. Usually, at the end of a trip there are tears, embraces, exchanges of addresses and emails, but after this river trip there was barely a handshake.

Creating harmony in an outdoor lifestyle, first and most importantly, is realizing and admitting to your lack of knowledge; this lack of knowledge, if exercised in the wilderness, then becomes your ineptness if things go wrong. And just as there are no real shortcuts through the wilderness, there are no shortcuts in the technical craftsmanship needed to master any skill.

Sand Skull by Hap Wilson.

Why doesn't he answer his emails?

ELEVEN
BUSH PLANES

I realized that if I had to choose, I would rather have birds than airplanes.

— Charles Lindbergh (1902–1974)

"Meet the plane at the public dock just outside Yellowknife, I'll be there at four o'clock," the pilot chimed over the phone, not very convincingly. He was already a day late. I had three clients with me, primed to run a photo shoot on the Coppermine River. Earlier that day while killing time at the Golden Arms Pub, I had bumped into a pilot who used to fly in Ontario with Lakeland Airways. I had flown with him on several occasions and he had moved back home where his father was an accountant in Yellowknife. He had come back home to fly with Air Tindy — a reputable charter service based out of Old Town.

"Who are you flying with?" he queried. "Bushwhack Bob," I told him a little reluctantly. "Good luck, you'll need it," the pilot said with disdain and a slight grin. I pried more information about Bushwhack Bob out of him than I felt comfortable with, careful not to let my clients overhear our conversation. Bushwhack, apparently, owed money to just about everybody in Yellowknife, and if he turned up in town, someone was going to skin him like a caribou and nail his hide to the door of the Explorer Hotel.

Workhorse of the North and ready for the pasture.

Beaver Airplane by Ingrid Zschogner.

Great … I had paid this guy up front to fly the four of us into the Coppermine. He had a DeHavilland Beaver and could do it in one flight he said. I had a couple of pakboats, folding/inflatable canoes that packed into hockey bags, and that would eliminate any external canoe loads. It was already past six o'clock when the plane finally arrived. When it arrived at the dock I noticed that the pontoons were under water. Every float plane has a red line maximum load indicator painted on each pontoon and these were well submerged, at least until Bushwhack Bob jumped on to the dock — all 280 pounds of him, smiling, cocky, unkempt, white shmutz crackling at the edge of his mouth. He flicked a cigarette butt into the lake. Five men clambered out of the plane, cursing, grabbing at their gear, making comments about the flight being one of the worst ever. Two men had to sit on top of the gear as there weren't enough seats in the plane to accommodate everyone. They were heading straight for the bar.

Even with all their gear out of the plane, the floats were still mostly submerged. Then I noticed that the mandatory call letters on the side of the fuselage had been whitewashed over. Someone arrived in a beat up truck with a forty-five-gallon drum of avgas in the back; it was Bob's assistant. He looked nervous and jittery and demanded that we help him pump the fuel into the plane. When we were finished, Bob and his sidekick jumped in the truck and took off. "I'll be back in two hours … gotta get some sleep," Bob said. "You guys can load 'er up."

We stood there dumbfounded, angry, hungry, and the sun was slipping over the horizon quickly. No reputable pilot ever lets the client load the plane on his own. Inside was a shambles; interior liners had pulled away from the fuselage walls, duct tape held the seats together, and on the floor beside the pilot's seat was an ashtray overflowing with butts, and it looked as if old vomit had crusted on the floor. The aroma was thick with sweat and mold. After loading the plane with our gear the max-line indicators on the pontoons were under water. *That can't be*, I thought … *any other Beaver could carry this load and its passengers without a problem.* The floats looked too small for the plane and were probably rife with leaks. After tracking down Bushwhack we told him that it didn't look safe enough to fly in his plane; we had already made other arrangements to fly out the next day with Air Tindy. He agreed to leave my refund at the hotel when we returned to Yellowknife two weeks later. Only half of which was returned a year later.

After contacting the NWT tourism authorities it turned out that Bushwhack had been flying with a suspended licence. There were several lawsuits pending against him. But the tourism department won't revoke his operating licence because, as I was informed by one of their senior agents, Bob "fills a void" in their marketing plan; that is, he operates an interior "eco-camp" and somehow manages to coerce top name photographers to base out of his remote facility. "It's good advertising for us, for the territory. The photographs get around," I was told. It didn't matter that his website was misleading, that he was a liar and a thief … it was good business for the province. So what if he had a few dozen disgruntled canoeist-clients who got screwed.

The pilot didn't look as if he were out of high school yet. He was nervous … I could tell by the way he was talking too much. He was sweating, leaning way too far forward and had a death grip on the controls. The floats on the Cessna 185 barely cleared the tops of the big pines that rimmed the higher ridges — too close for comfort. The hills were abrupt here, with sheer cliffs and deep gorges. It was foggy, and the ceiling steadily declining, but instead of putting down safely on a lake and waiting for the weather to clear, he pushed on. The base manager wanted to keep to the tight schedule as there was already a backlog of clients waiting to fly in. And this pilot was lost.

I could tell he had no idea where we were. I knew the area but it was even hard for me to get a site bearing with such a low ceiling. The plane wasn't equipped with a GPS, not that it would have helped much, anyway. I opened my map and showed him where we were, already several degrees off course. Trees loomed directly in front of the plane and the pilot pulled back on the stick to clear the ridge. By the time we landed everyone had just about pissed themselves. By the end of the season this pilot would crash his plane into a three-hundred-foot communications tower, killing all four occupants.

The pilot was obviously stoned. Worse yet, it was nearly dark and we were in the midst of a terrific summer thunderstorm. I had made the radio call to the Natural Resources base office earlier that day to pick me and my crew up from Wakimika Lake, hopefully before the storms hit. No government planes were available and they wouldn't have flown in this weather, anyway, I was told. The private charter company would pick us up instead. After ten days cutting trails we were all exhausted, bug-bit, and looking forward to getting out of the bush. We knew that the private airways would fly in just about any weather for the money. They had a reputation. They also had a reputation for hiring novice young pilots.

It was raining hard when the Beaver aircraft landed. I didn't know this pilot well, just the fact that he hadn't worked long for the air service. He seemed inordinately cocky last time I flew with him and nobody on board felt comfortable at all. Now, when he got out of the plane after mooring it along the shore, he started cursing as he loaded our gear, tossing it any which way into the stow behind the rear seat. It wasn't just the rain, there was an obvious tension protracted from a disturbed pilot with some kind of grudge. He never stopped talking once he landed; only it wasn't the usual chatter between pilot and client, it was a long string of declarations and grievances, groaning and whining about his life and his job and how everything sucked. Lightning seared the now barely visible landscape around us, obscured by pelting rain and waning evening light. The storm showed no signs of letting up. The pilot didn't care — he was switched on and bemused by his own ramblings, intoxicated and unpredictable. We were afraid to say anything, afraid to get in the plane. But we had little choice but to carry on with this macabre scene.

"Yeah, this is my last flight," the pilot blurted out. What the fuck did that mean? Was it everyone's last flight? I tried talking with him but he wouldn't let me get a word in. I asked him what he meant by what he said.

"The prick fired me this afternoon ... said this was my last flight then I'm done for the summer." Another barrage of obscenities. Great — a pilot with hostilities, and he's looped out, and we're flying through a thunderstorm. We sat motionless in our seats, afraid to say anything lest the pilot turn on us. For the next half-hour I thought we were all going to die — not from the threat of being hit by lightning but by the acrobatic antics of a man possessed with nothing left to live for. "Watch this," he'd say, letting out a shrill hoorah and we'd drop into a vertical nose dive earthward, and then pull up in a steep ascent, nearly stalling out, fanning out in a half-spin. All this with two canoes strapped to the pontoons. This was crazy. Even if we complained to the owner it would be to no purpose — this pilot was history, anyway. By the time we reached town the pilot had settled down, ranting changing to half sobs about losing his girlfriend to a buddy back home. Silence: except for the drone of the engine as we taxied in to the airways dock.

Next day there was a fresh young pilot, full of smiles, loading gear onto the plane. He was to fly the Cessna 180 until he felt comfortable with the Beaver. Two weeks later, on a windy but perfectly clear day, he crashed the Beaver into the side of a steep ridge, the plane bursting into flames, instantly killing all four aboard.

I made a satellite phone call to the air service in Yellowknife to pick our group up at Lynx Lake near the headwater of the Thelon River in the Northwest Territories. They would pick us up just after six in the evening. It had been a tough trip, wind bound for over a week, extreme late summer weather causing us to change our itinerary and abandon descending the Thelon River. Instead, because we were unable to paddle, we trekked the open tundra in search of muskoxen and tundra wolves, hiking kilometres each day, the wind never letting up until the very last day. Even though we experienced a part of the beautiful headwater region of the Thelon that few people ever see, we all felt a little disappointed that the river adventure was thwarted, and for some they knew they would never be back again.

I called again when the plane was two hours past the scheduled pickup time. Lucky that evening could last up until midnight out here on the tundra. I wasn't too worried. The Cessna Caravan landed on the beach at ten o'clock — four hours past due time. It was a three-hour flight back to Yellowknife and the pilot was anxious to get us out of there. We had to help him unload two forty-five-gallon drums of avgas for another air service. These had to be carefully rolled down the pontoon steps onto the pontoon, and then skidded down planks into the water. One of the drum bung-caps was loose and fuel spilled out (also letting water into the submerged barrel) and we quickly rolled it up onto the beach out of the lake. It was mayhem. There was now an oily fuel slick running down the steps of the Cessna and branching out into the bay; people slipped as they climbed the greasy steps and found their seats. The smell of fuel was thick inside. I helped the pilot load the gear into the back of the plane. He looked nervous.

"We have four more people to pick up," the pilot told me. What … we already had a full load with ten people on board? Four Norwegian canoeists had decided to come out early and had made the call to the air service to come and pick them up. They never had a GPS with them and were lost in the labyrinth of lakes about one hundred air kilometres west of our location. They were told to light a smoky fire so the plane could spot them. The air service would also double their money on the back-haul by loading these guys on to our flight manifest, saving big on the fuel costs.

We spotted them after flying ever-tightening circles around the presumed location. There was no smoke to indicate the fire from a distance but we did notice the flames as it was now past dusk and near midnight, the sun having set about an hour earlier. We landed and I helped the pilot get the four men and their gear and Pakboats on board. There was a ton of gear and they were all big men. Huge duffels were piled down the middle aisle, infused with smoke which now blended with the smell of spilt fuel and old sweat.

"This is crazy," the pilot whispered to me before we climbed in off the float. I didn't answer him. I could see he was nervous. We still had a two-hour flight back to Yellowknife and the sun had long since departed. Only the Norwegians chatted amongst themselves, elated that they were plucked out of the wilderness and were heading home.

We landed without incident. The result of the spilled fuel barrels at the beach on Lynx Lake where avgas was dropped off for another air service, ended up in a nasty lawsuit. The fuel barrels had taken on water through unsecured bungs. The other air service was never notified of the potential spoiled fuel. When their plane went in to retrieve our canoes and refueled with the spoiled avgas the engine had a "flame-out" on take-off and had to put down roughly on the windiest section of lake. For two days, the pilot and his assistant tried desperately to keep the plane from crashing into shore rocks, meanwhile staving off the threat of hypothermia in near freezing temperatures.

High gravel banks oozing from once frozen permafrost lined both sides of the Coppermine River in Nunavut. There was nowhere to lunch as the shore was a scrabble of rock and course willow; eating in the canoe was an option but we wanted to get out and stretch our legs. Fifty vertical feet up, out of view, the tundra heath spread out endlessly; there was usually enough level moss matt to spread out and eat lunch on. We randomly selected a beaching site for the canoes, grabbed the lunch pack, and scrambled up the steep bank. What we saw at the top was disturbing.

Out of sheer coincidence we had chosen the exact site of a Cessna 180 crash site. The burned out fuselage and wings were a grim testimony of a flight gone awry. Pilot error or mechanical malfunction, bad weather or just bad luck, there was a story here that demanded an explanation.

Flying in to the trailhead is often part of the adventure and, for the number of flights made, there are few accidents. Getting in to a remote start point quickly by air can cut days, sometimes weeks of travel time off the schedule but there are enough close calls and deaths to warrant some trepidation when it comes to selecting an air service. Just as there are many reputable air charter services, there are as many operators and pilots who fly by the skin of their teeth. Just like guides, pilots can make poor judgment calls and there have been times that I've witnessed the pilot's ego framing the potency of his ability to appraise situations and put everyone at risk. There really *are* no old, **bold** pilots as the saying goes. Northern charter services conscript young pilots who are eager to chock up air mile time — to the owner, rookie pilots come cheap and are expendable. There's no shortage of fly boys available to commandeer any number of aging floatplanes out there. A few noticeable traits that you may want to be wary of when you slide in next to the pilot with the hangover from the night before, or the pilot who just got jilted by the bosses daughter:

1. The pilot suddenly slides forward on the edge of his seat.
2. He grips the steering controls too hard.
3. Beads of sweat appear on his forehead on a cool day.
4. He curses while manoeuvring.
5. Pilot asks you where he is.
6. He keeps clearing his throat but doesn't speak.
7. There is duct tape holding things together.
8. A roach-clip is stuck to the flight log.
9. There's a mickey of rye in the door pocket.
10. There's oil dripping from the engine cowling.
11. The pilot pumps out floats on takeoff and landing.
12. The pilot asks you to load the plane.

I'll keep flying even though I've seen it all. I am more selective now, though, and I'll ask the charter service how many hours flying time my pilot has, especially if it looks as if he hasn't started shaving yet. And when I'm up there, heart racing a little faster than normal, I sometimes forget that I'm not a religious man and I utter a silent prayer. So far so good, I say to myself when we land. The hard-pack trail looks better than ever, and the pitch of the canoe over the waves is comforting and earthly.

Fairy Point, Lake Missinaibi pictographs — a sacred place.

PART THREE
PATHWAY TO NIRVANA:
THE SPIRIT OF PLACE

The real voyage of discovery consists not in seeking new landscapes but in having new eyes.
— Marcel Proust (1871–1922)

Beauty always has a price attached to it; we either want to own it, exercise power over it, squander it, or lay waste to it. As is often the case, places of aesthetic pleasure have great alluring qualities to the adventurer; they also have a protective mechanism built into their personalities. The harshness of the environment may be a deterrent for some travellers or the level of whitewater too difficult and dangerous for others. These are physical characteristics that could define almost any northern Canadian river, mountain, or trail. Sometimes there is a deeper story about a place that beguiles any rational explanation or reason.

Artery Lake pictographs — a teaching place.

TWELVE
BLOODVEIN

The important thing is not to stop questioning. Curiosity has its own reasons for existing. One cannot help but be in awe when he contemplates the mysteries of eternity, of life, of the marvellous structure of reality. It is enough if one tries merely to comprehend a little of this mystery every day. Never lose a holy curiosity.
— Albert Einstein (1879–1955)

T he bison image remains a mystery, like the paint itself, used to immortalize ancient thought and the transcripts of a healer-shaman. So, what was the bonding agent? Fish oil? Egg albumen from gull eggs, or some sort of Neolithic acrylic? Or, was it perhaps the blood essence of the stone people — the *memegwishiwok* — proffered to the artist for some sublime ceremony, emblazoned on the rock face of granite by sheer magic? And, how is it that two almost identical bison images, painted long before Euro-travel connected the two continents, show up on rock walls thousands of kilometres apart? Coincidence? Or perhaps some metaphysical soul transfer — a telepathic information exchange between shamans that could transcend any boundary, any distance, any dimension?

I'm referring, of course, to the internationally renowned pictographs (rock paintings) found along the Bloodvein River. This heritage waterway wends its way through the woodland caribou country of northwest Ontario and east-central Manitoba. There are at least twelve known pictograph sites, each one imparting a lesson, possibly a warning, to those who venture close enough, to gaze into their own soul and immortality. These rock scriptures go far beyond the whimsy of present-day, rock-cut graffiti; alive with spiritual energy, they may well be the conduit, or portal, to the spirit world itself.

Once an agnostic about such things, my rather limited view of the spirit realm blossomed after my initial ghost experience some years ago, which took place while renovating an old farmhouse in the Laurentians. My wife and I were treated to an unexpected social call by the long-departed first lady of the century-old dwelling. It was an eerie and frightening experience, at first, but the everlasting and profound effect the visitation had on the way I now view life — and beyond — was remarkably liberating. I no longer felt encumbered by doubt. My own existence and station on Mother Earth took on a new pithiness. Patrick Giesler, anthropologist and parapsychologist professor for the University of Chicago — a good friend of mine — has studied the paranormal, cult worship, zombiism, and shamanic practices worldwide. "Of any psychic or paranormal experience, one should not fight it, but relax into it," he remarks. "This is the door opening for soul travel … you just have to learn how to walk through it."

I began studying shamanic practice and North American Native theology, almost to the point of obsession. I was particularly fascinated by rock art, something that white anthropologists with strong Christian persuasions seemed to dismiss as pagan renderings of little religious importance. Archaeologists interpreted the images as art, wholly from a white perspective, assuming they knew what they meant. Only the shaman healer and his students held the secret to the paintings. And there is an omnipresent spiritual force at these sites, where the shaman-teacher-healer practised his or her trade, where the physical world as we know it melds easily with the spirit world.

Could there be an evil power at play here? Malevolence spawned from the depths of some primal religion? A vengeance? Visitations to such sacrosanct places were not allowed, at one time, unless in the accompaniment of a healer-shaman. Any visit would require the offering of tobacco. Today, little or no respect or reverence is paid to these sites other than mild curiosity, as paddlers snap pictures, fondle the rock and even scratch their own names among the rock effigies. The practice of leaving a tobacco offering, at least, if not taking a moment for a prayer, or asking permission to pass by in safety, is not common enough.

Further to the north, along Manitoba's Grass River, there is a wall of impressive rock paintings on Tramping Lake. Two local mine workers from the nearby community took a motorboat out to see the ancient drawings on rock and left their own signatures painted over the pictographs. Within the month, both men were dead — one in a violent car crash, the other in a mining accident. On the Missinaibi River in Ontario, where more than thirty-four people died over a period of fourteen years, half the deaths occurred at spiritual sites. Coincidence?

Miskowiskibi — the Bloodvein — best represents the drama of place, both geographically and spiritually. Flowing from Knox Lake in Ontario, just northwest of the town of Red Lake, the river tumbles recklessly over abrupt granite ledges on its three-hundred-kilometre journey to Lake Winnipeg, west toward the setting sun, west toward the sea of prairie grass, spilling into the geographic umbilicus of North America. Gentle current drifts between tumultuous chutes and rapids, actually making upstream travel possible — one of the prime factors that popularized the Bloodvein as a Native travel route, dating back as far as nine thousand years ago when Paleo cultures followed the retreating glaciers as the boreal-upland forests flourished. Archaeological exploits along the river have literally unearthed a plethora of burial mounds, middens, entire village sites, skeletal remains, chipped stone, pottery, worked copper and, most important, the richest conglomeration of rock-art sites found in the country.

After being detained in Red Lake for three days because of interior wildfires burning in the vicinity of the Bloodvein, I was able to work my way slowly toward the headwater, trying not to think of the fires as some kind of prophetic caution. Since its inception as a Canadian Heritage

River, and because it bisected both Ontario's Woodland Caribou and Manitoba's Atikaki (A-tick-a-key) parks, the Bloodvein corridor had been documented by the bureaucrats for everything except recreational travel. Government foresters prescribed boundaries (some arbitrarily configured) so that the hungry needs of the logging companies could be assuaged before anything else.

The trip on the Bloodvein was part of my Manitoba wilderness guidebook project, and much of the study material I used was not readily available to the public; and with good reason. More and more graffiti had been showing up on top of easily accessed pictographs, but since my research was purely investigative, I was privy to all archaeological findings. I agreed not to give exact locations in my Manitoba guidebook of any pictographs not already publicly identified in printed material.

Gaining access to the Bloodvein demands a somewhat dogged persistence. Dealing with bugs and recent burn-overs where blowdowns littered the lengthy portage trails leaves you feeling a bit daunted. But as with any wilderness river, the necessary grunt work generally means that few people have trekked the upper reaches. In fact, with the Bloodvein, most paddlers opt to fly in to Artery Lake on the Ontario–Manitoba border, where it's a much easier two-week paddle to Lake Winnipeg, thereby eliminating the more than eight kilometres of ankle-wrenching portaging they would have endured had they started their trip at Red Lake. The downside of this option, assuming that Native cultural stuff is important, is that paddlers miss half of the twelve pictograph sites.

I picked up a client group at Barclay Lake, about thirty kilometres east of the Manitoba border. I explained the importance of approaching the pictograph sites with caution, and that I would make a tobacco offering at each one, as I had been accustomed to doing, and that anyone wishing to leave prayers could do so. Not everyone agrees with my sentiment, or cares to share the seriousness of approaching such places with reverence, for whatever personal reason — religious faith being one of them. All usually agree to the practice, if only out of respect for the group dynamic.

On day two, I slipped behind the group while photographing a mink with a dead merganser duck clenched in its jaw. The others were heading down a deep bay, off the main route of the river, at the extreme northeast end of Mary's Lake, making rather good time to the base of a high cliff where I told them we would find a pictograph. It was dead calm, and I easily caught up to the group who were now collected below the immense rock face, and the painting of red ochre and magic was as visible as the day it had been created. It portrayed a lone shaman, a powerful image — a simple cartoon-like figure. Instead of the usual body outline and projecting arms and legs, the torso had been painted in — an indication that there was strong energy here.

I had the same feeling well over me as I had when I met my first ghost — a sense of dread, prickly skin, slight nausea, or like when I walk into an old dwelling that has a particular resident malevolent energy and I feel an overwhelming need to get out. I had allowed our group to approach the site in such a manner as to evoke the wrath of the resident spirit entity. I had been forewarned about this particular pictograph as one of particular omnipotence. A commanding southwest wind, without warning, slammed into our little flotilla of boats, crashing gunwales together in a moment of angry mayhem. It was time to leave. The reproach came in the guise of a rogue windstorm that precipitated a hasty retreat. A quick offering of tobacco seemed to be a senseless gesture, like closing the gate after the lion had escaped.

The wind persisted. Ominous clouds rolled in like massive bulwarks, and we made a quick camp at the edge of a small rapid. Within fifteen minutes of setting up our tents, a difficult enough process in such heavy wind, a summer storm hit us with such vehemence it seemed the forces of Nature had quite outdone themselves. Trees toppled around us while gale-force winds pummeled the boreal landscape like a heavy fist upon its back; lightning seared around the makeshift camp, stabbing randomly at the bent forest while rain whipped at us in horizontal sheets. We had no protection — it was too dangerous to stay in the tents because trees were coming down all around us, and the rain fly had ripped away from its moorings. The sound was deafening. We chose to stand as a group at the edge of a copse of young spruce trees which afforded a modicum of cover and the least likelihood of getting struck by lightning.

And as quickly as it had come, it was gone. And the evening sun probed the remnant clouds for openings through which to cast a surreal patchwork glow over the drenched landscape — an ocherous brilliance. The only sound was the spent rain drops filtering through the leaves of the forest.

Nearby was another pictograph site; in fact, it was the most celebrated rock-art site along the Bloodvein, and the prime time to view it was under the patina of evening light just before the sun set. Everyone in the group, including the skeptical, literally jumped into their canoes after I had suggested we make some kind of amends with the river. And as a devout Christian might enter a place of worship, we approached the pictographs slowly and quietly, each canoe party ready to divulge some sort of personal offering. Tobacco pouches were passed around.

This was the famous bison site, and as famed archaeologist Selwyn Dewdney remarks, "The site is perhaps a hundred miles north of the parklands where the bison herds once roamed; but the artist shows familiarity with the animal that supports either frequent hunting excursions southward, or his own southern origin."

Halfway across the world there is a similar bison image, depicted with circled hooves, and as much an anomaly there as the painting at Artery Lake, Manitoba. Coincidence seems unlikely. Shamanism and the art of healing souls are the fundamentals of an ancient religion and practice that predates Christianity by twenty thousand years. Not a black art, as branded by modern religious scholars, shamanic faith bonds itself to the rhythm of the Earth and is the basis of North American Native beliefs and healing practices. The possibility of early healers having the ability to transcend known planes of existence, to vault their spiritual selves through some kind of time-place portal, to be able to exchange wisdom with other shamans linked like some kind of spiritual Internet, is not fantasy or mythology or simple campfire story … at least to this writer.

The granite wall absorbed the incident evening light, turning from pale to reddish yellow. The dark waters of the Bloodvein and the thick moss and boreal crown above the face of the rock framed and highlighted the magical, mysterious paintings, like a Precambrian holograph display. There was not a word spoken amongst us lest the charm of the spell be broken. Our canoes drifted as if suspended between two dimensions, drifting like the ephemeral light, hovering momentarily, bathing the moment in illusory calm.

The sun dropped below the fringe of trees on the opposite shore, leaving the teaching site in evening sameness and shadow. The magic was gone, the latch on the door once again bolted. None of us made a move to paddle the three kilometres back to the campsite. Our earlier transgressions against the spirit world had been purged. It was an experience we would all remember — an event in our lives, however enigmatic, that in some way brings us closer to the answer.

The Bloodvein River conveys a message understood by very few, even to the remnant Saulteaux Ojibwa who have been assimilated into the world of consumerism and may have forgotten the old ways and who now grasp at the tattered edges of their own culture. Few resident Anishnabe venture this far upriver — a two-week trek by canoe. I resign myself to that place of bewilderment, like most others who travel its waters, play in the rapids and walk the nastawgan trails, getting caught up in the waterplay and the landscape and the camaraderie, and such vain pleasures that appease the physical senses. But I hope, as I continue to visit these places and revel in the sanctity of ancient wisdom, that I may someday understand more about what went on here, in the mind of the teacher who left us such cryptic lessons on stone.

Trickster at Campsite by Hap Wilson.

The payhunsuk — the playful trickster.

THIRTEEN
THUNDERHOUSE

The Devil has made off with one of the packs!
— Native companion of explorer Phillipe Turner
at Thunderhouse Falls portage, 1781

Canadians, generally speaking, are known for their rational, even-keel approach to the supernatural. Even some of our great writers have denied that Canada is home to ghosts, pixies, and monsters of world-class stature. Certainly, Indian mythology and legend have become the stuff of children's bedtime stories, but underlying the surface fluff is a Pandora's Box of hardcore demonkind.

Their existence has long been repudiated, dismissed, and sublimated by science, logic, Christianity, and cultural disconnection from the natural world. Our fears, however, remain. Demons thrive yet in the deep recesses of the forest and our minds. Mythology played an important role in the everyday life of the woodland Aboriginal people who believed that everything living or inanimate had a soul, a purpose, and a voice.

After thirty-five years of extensive research, personal observations, and experiences along the trail, I can report that I have witnessed many strange events — some of which have been precursors to mysterious deaths and disappearances. Oddly enough, an increasing number of canoe deaths within the Canadian wilds have occurred at places of "harmonic convergence" — specific sites where the corporeal world (the world as we know it in material means or "the land of upright life" to the Anishnabeg) melds easily with the incorporeal, or spirit world. Most often located at places of peculiar geophysical nature (pinnacles, waterfalls, cliff faces), they are strikingly beautiful, pristine, and isolated (getting less so as industry encroaches and destroys wilderness). Medicine men and women of the Medewewin Society (shamans dedicated to healing and soul therapy) used these sacred sites for ceremonies over the centuries. Drums, chants, and even hallucinogens (frequently peyote and magic mushrooms) helped to induce the shamanic trance and soul travel. No one was allowed to pass these places without leaving a gift for the resident spirit, generally tobacco or a medicine bundle. In return, the spirit would allow safe passage to either a physical or metaphysical destination. Thunderhouse Falls is one of those places.

Thunderhouse Gorge is probably the most acclaimed attraction of the Missinaibi River for its remarkable beauty, if for no other reason. But there is much more to it than simple visual appeal. Geologically, it represents the bold interface between the rocky Precambrian Shield and the James Bay Lowlands, exposing one of the thickest, continuous stratigraphic displays of early Precambrian gneisses and migmatites (striated and folded rock probing almost half a kilometre below the steep canyon walls). Mother Earth herself, exposed and vulnerable.

Thunderhouse also marks the rapid transition between Shield boreal forest and the vast, impenetrable slough of muskeg and spruce that runs to the sea. During the fur trade era it represented a monumental navigational obstacle fifteen kilometres long, establishing itself as a "rendezvous" point of exchange between Moose Factory rivermen and the voyageurs of the interior who came from as far away as Lake Superior and the Michipicoten Post.

But by far the most intriguing quality of Thunderhouse is its representation as a place of shamanic practice, in a physical and spiritual rationale. It once marked the division between western Ojibway and eastern James Bay Cree territories. Shamans from both cultures performed ceremonies here. The Conjuring House Rock — a pillar of impervious stone rising seventy-five feet out of the depths of the canyon below the falls, resembles the very shape of the Algonkian shaman's sacred "shaking tent." It is little wonder that early Native healers and seekers practised ceremonio-religious rites at this place.

It is purported that the shamans collected magic mushrooms — "shrooms" — that grew along the portage trail, for use in their ceremonies. When I first visited Thunderhouse, and carried my packs over the sixteen-hundred-metre trail, the first thing I noticed was the abundance of *Amanita muscaria*; easily recognized by its large rust-orange, white-spotted cap and phallic stem. Red squirrels had been collecting the shrooms, and pieces were either eaten out of them or chunks carried up trees and stuffed in the crotches of branches. *Amanita muscaria* is considered an edible mushroom but depending on the dosage, it could be lightly hallucinogenic. It was used as a winter tonic enhancer and relaxant (in mild doses), and as a hallucinogen (in heavier doses) for ceremonial use. However, *muscaria* does not have the potency and negative effects of the *Psilocybe* mushrooms. *Psilocybe* mushrooms can easily be mistaken for deadly shrooms, whereas the *Amanita muscaria* is recognizable and autonomous.

The use of magic mushrooms has been verified through archaeological studies and research; evidence for their ceremonial use goes back thousands of years. Several Mesolithic rock paintings from Tassili n'Ajjer (a prehistoric North African site) have been identified as depicting shamanic use of mushrooms. Increased use and dosage carries the possibility of a spiritual event known as "ego death," whereby the user loses the sense of boundaries between their physical body and the environment, creating a sort of perceived (or real) universal unity — an out-of-body experience. Actual death doesn't occur, although it is said that the once the soul leaves the body on a journey, the physical being is at risk (from cold, hypothermia, animal attack, falling, injury, etc.). Usually, there is a "keeper of the body" nearby to tend to the shaman's physical body while the soul is travelling. Poet Dylan Thomas remarks, "… after the first death, there is no other," which could be translated to mean that once the shaman gets the hang of it, the door into the spirit world opens more readily.

The spirit presence at Thunderhouse is very strong with dual personalities. It can be very angry and dangerous; or elusive, playful, and mischievous. As mentioned in a previous chapter, several people have died here, even experienced canoeists who got lured into the rapids above the falls. Nebaunaubaequae, to the Anshnabeg, was a symbol of the incorporeal nature of the water, appearing to man as a woman, and to woman as a man, seducing or enticing the victim and then drowning them. At Thunderhouse, Neb may very well be manifesting itself as a luring water spirit, tempting canoeists to run the rapids instead of taking the safe route along the portage. It was easy to get caught up in the water-play. Out of curiosity, I solo canoed down the rapids leading to the falls that had been the cause of five deaths and multiple close calls over the years. I've run many rapids, rapids more difficult and technical than these, but there was something deathly mysterious about this run. I felt that it had an aura, a drawing effect that pulled you deep into the centre channel away from shore — a dangerous place to be in high water as it was difficult to extricate yourself safely away from the current pulling you toward the falls. Here you could see the calm of the pool at the bottom of the rapids, where the portage trail was marked on the maps — a trail that didn't exist — and the lure of an easy carry around the gorge was appealing. The falls remains invisible, inaudible, until your canoe passes through a narrow cut in the rock and the river pulls hard to the left as if crouching, waiting for you around the corner of a building. Once there you can't escape unless you're very lucky; if you swamp, the current is too strong to fight against … and Nebaunaubaequae claims another victim.

The Paueehnsuk also dwell here; little creatures that reside along the rocky shores who emerge in the evening to play along the dark corridors of the forest. They sit beside your tent at night and enter your dreams, trying to negate the powerful energy and influence of Nebaunaubaequae by sending you messages and warnings. Sometimes they just like to play tricks. Maybe you portaged your camping gear and set up your tent near the precipice overlooking the canyon, and left your canoe at the trailhead thinking you could run the rapids in the morning. Maybe you had a dream that night, something unsettling that made you change your mind about

Shaman by Hap Wilson.

Thunderhouse shaman — a place of strong divination.

running the rapids above the falls, and you ended up making the long portage, all the time trying to think of why or what changed your mind.

Over the past several years I have spoken with individuals who have had extraordinary or preternatural experiences at Thunderhouse. I was astounded at the numbers who have had things happen to them that were unexplainable, bizarre, eerie, and wonderful. Strange occurrences have been recorded as far back as 1781, in the journals of Phillipe Turner, who blamed his Indian porteurs of misplacing a pack while portaging around Thunderhouse Falls. White explorers had no time for Native superstitions, yet his guides insisted that a "devil" had stolen it. Most recent accounts of mysterious happenings, oddly enough, have focused on disappearing equipment. It happened to me.

It was my first trip down the river and I had a mid-size party of clients. I was vaguely aware of the deaths that had occurred at the falls, and of its historical import as a spiritual gathering place. Everything was systematic; we portaged the gear to the campsite and set up at the gorge site across from the Conjuring Rock. We then went back to the trailhead and portaged the four canoes and stacked them at the far end of the carry, just below the gorge on a bedrock terrace. We kept the canoes back from the edge of the river, about fifty feet, leaving my canoe on the outside so I could come back later and take it out to scout for firewood. I remember pushing my lifejacket and paddles under my canoe. High water had left driftwood in remnant piles along the outside bend of the gorge. The current was strong, funneling through the gorge just upstream and pushing hard downriver toward Hell's Gate. The movement of water through the rock walls of the canyon created its own eerie wind — light, cool, and pulsing with the surge and flow of the current. There was always uneasiness here.

We ate dinner with an hour left of evening light. The alpenglow on the canyon wall across the river ascended as the sun slipped behind the trees of the campsite. At these places I keep a vigilant eye on the clients; there was a hundred-foot cliff only metres from the pitched tents and, after a couple of shots of rum, the day's wear and tear can make them careless. Nobody had moved from the campsite since we carried the canoes across, and I knew no other canoeists had come through that day, as the portage trail went right by the campsite. I wanted to check on the canoes; for some reason I had the impulse to walk to the end of the portage.

Walking the half kilometre to the end of the trail I saw that the canoes were still neatly stacked. I was about to turn around and go back when I took a second look. Something definitely was different. I walked over to the canoes and saw that mine was gone — even the lifejacket and two paddles. All my clients were accounted for and no one had come down to the river, and no other paddlers had come through. I walked to the river edge and looked downriver but saw no sign of my canoe. It was a seventeen-foot, eighty-pound expedition canoe — it wouldn't just blow off the site on its own. Even with a freak wind funnel, it was too heavy. *And where were my paddles and lifejacket?*

I grabbed another canoe and borrowed a client's lifejacket and put it on. All I could do was to paddle downriver and hope my canoe had gotten hung up on a rock; it was unlikely, though, because of the current and rapids that now went on for at least fifteen kilometres. It seemed hopeless. What was I going to do with one less canoe? What was I going to tell the group? I slipped the canoe into the water and was about to shove off, heading downstream, when something caught my eye upstream. It was my canoe, and it was moving of its own volition, up against the current, rounding a bend out of sight into the canyon. I had the feeling that someone was watching me. I looked around but nobody was there.

I paddled hard against the current, trying to keep to the backwater eddy and the sheerline that ran along the inside of the canyon bend. I caught up to my canoe just before the conjuring rock, grabbed the gunwale and looked inside. My two paddles and lifejacket were lying neatly on the bottom of the canoe; there was no water splash or bilge-water, just a dry, neat canoe with an apparent mind of its own. It was possessed.

I towed it back and restacked the two canoes with the others. Just to be sure, I tied the canoes together with a painter and secured it to a tree nearby. It was nearly dark and I hurried back to the campsite. I didn't tell the others. It was my secret. I did ask if anyone had been down to the canoes earlier but everyone had been married to their evening cigars and whisky and warm campfire. I wanted to tell the others but couldn't. They wouldn't have believed me, anyway.

I have been back to Thunderhouse since, both with other clients as well as on my own. By then I had learned some of its secrets and made sure my canoes were either left at the campsite, or secured by ropes at trail's end. People started sharing their stories with me during the time I was writing my guidebook about the river and researching the deaths, and the stories were as peculiar as my own. Several canoe parties had lost at least a canoe, or some part of their kit and gear, for no apparent reason or sloppy woodsmanship — *it just disappeared.* Others complained about disturbing dreams, voices from the woods at night, and even sightings of ghosts and other creatures at the edge of the campsite. A friend of mine stayed at Thunderhouse for two nights with her husband and confessed that she was never so terrified in her life. Each night was an ordeal of frightening dreams, and when she lay awake, the night sounds were unrecognizable and unearthly.

My last solo trip down the river was the most memorable for me. It was late September and frost was already forming on the overturned canoe each morning. There was ice in the tea pail, and the occasional snow shower. There was nobody else on the lower river at the time, just sandhill cranes and Canada geese. I had planned to stay at Thunderhouse for three days and nights, hoping to extract some of its mystery, to perhaps prove that the strange occurrences were simply explainable coincidences. When I arrived at Thunderhouse there was a light rain falling, and it was cold and windy. I sat on the precipice overlooking the conjuring rock, and in my own way requested permission to be there. Sitting thirty metres above the cauldron below, from the campsite perch, I could look at the rapids above the falls on a level plane before the river tumbled into the gorge. In the canyon, huge piles of refuse timber had nestled into the crevices of the walls, suspended ten metres above the diminished, passive late-summer flow. Swirling eddies and whirlpools cast out ribbons of spiralling white foam.

I visited my favourite spot on the rocks, next to the narrow second chute where the full spirit of the Missinaibi is compressed and compelled to expose itself. Between the upper falls and where I stood was a temporary pool — a foaming, pulsating maelstrom of liquid energy, surging in half-metre rhythms. The rain transposed the multi-coloured stones and rock into a gallery of glistening art treasures, like a high-gloss lacquer brings out the grain in a piece of wood. The more resistant rock stood out like veins gorged with blood; potholes, deep and sometimes conjoined were now exposed in low water — strange recesses with a prize in their bellies of a rounded stone; glacially-carved fissures, and deep grottos pockmarked the walls of this luminous art gallery.

I stood at the edge of the cliff once again and dropped some tobacco into the canyon. The wind took it and moved it in gentle circles, scattering the gift along the cliff wall and as far down as the river. I touched the rock with my hands, felt the wind on my face, and breathed the damp air. Most of the time I would just sit and listen and watch. For three days and nights, by the campfire, I listened to the rush of water through the canyon; loud but not so loud that I couldn't hear the flying squirrels gliding about the trees above my head.

I had dreams; even dreams that I could remember, and none of them were apocalyptic or threatening. There was no malevolent spirit living here, not for me, anyway, but there was an energy that commanded authority and respect. I always felt that someone, or some*thing*, was watching me the whole time I was there. And I waited and watched and hoped for some little bit of magic to happen. But it didn't. Maybe it was happening all around me and I was a part of it and didn't realize it. Isolation without extraneous human interaction is a liberating experience; it also allows the mind to wander and absorb each nuance of the surroundings, without interruption or obligation. I wondered what *muscaria* mushrooms would taste like mixed in with my rice and beans.

Trail companion.

FOURTEEN
RIVER OF FIRE

It is with our passions, as it is with fire and water; they are good servants but bad masters.
— Aesop (620–560 B.C.)

"Let's get the hell out of here NOW!" Hodding was yelling at Andy to get back into the canoe. "LOOK AT THE FIRE ... WE'VE GOT TO MOVE OR WE'RE TOAST!"

Russell and I were two hundred metres beyond in our canoe taking pictures of the fire while Andy had pulled his canoe up to shore at the end of the rapids to take a piss ... that's when we heard Hodding screaming at the top of his lungs to get moving.

"Christ, this is bad," I thought aloud. We had just finished running Nine Bar Rapids, a notorious 3.5-kilometre-long, hair-raising rollercoaster ride — a gnarly class 3 or 4 canoe eater. We ran the left side, eddying out twice to scout bends, and finished by dropping over a two-metre ledge, very nearly getting stuck in the hydraulic backwash. It was a fifty-foot drop — the type of rapid you can't scout — and wide, with no discernable channel, steep enough to obscure what you were running beyond a quarter of a kilometre. If that wasn't enough to get the adrenalin flowing, the entire north shore of the river was being engulfed in a conflagration the size of Prince Edward Island.

Russ and I sat in our canoe, completely enthralled by the towering flames that crowned at least two kilometres of river horizon, forming the leading edge of the wildfire. That's when we heard the roar — or rather felt it — above the din of the rapids. It sounded like a powerful freight train barrelling toward us, and we were standing on the tracks. The fire was consuming boreal forest at an alarming rate, moving almost twice as fast as we could possibly paddle. It wasn't the explosive flames so much as the threat of smoke engulfing us before we could get downriver to safety. We had been dodging wildfires for days, so bad at times that we had to brush burning and smoking debris off our clothing and canoe spray-skirts; we ran rapids while the shore vegetation burst into columns of fire and smoke, keeping just far enough offshore where it was safe. In places the fire had jumped the river and was burning on both sides. The current pull of the Seal was strong, drawing us further into the fire at a steady twelve kilometres per hour. But each day the wind miraculously carried the thick smoke straight up or away from the river, allowing us to sneak by unscathed. At worst, we had to tie wet bandanas across our faces to make it easier to breathe.

And now, sitting in our canoes dumbstruck, with the fire burning so fiercely, the air became saturated with burnt debris; a wall of black smoke descended on the surface of the rapids, just upstream, rolling toward us like a billowing, flowing tsunami. It was one of those moments when you feel that whatever you do would be futile. We had pushed our luck ... and now our luck had run out.

We paddled hard to keep just ahead of the deadly wall of smoke and to avoid being showered with scorched spruce needles. The river became a greasy pool of soot; the sun was blotted out and the day was transformed into an eerie orange twilight. Luckily, the rapids trailed out in a long series of swifts and shallow riffs that gave us just enough speed to outrun the fire. We paddled for our lives.

There was an Environment Canada water-monitoring shed about three kilometres downriver from Nine Bar Rapids and we headed there to catch our breath. Once inside the cabin we sat for only two minutes before hearing a volley of explosions. Not far from the confluence of the two channels around Great Island, about a kilometre from Nine Bar, was a 1950s mining camp. The company had shut down and left the camp intact, including having abandoned a fully stocked dynamite shed. We had originally planned to explore the camp for artifacts but the fire thwarted our side trip; now the camp was being razed, remnant blasting caps and charges were igniting, adding sharp retorts above the low rumble of the not so distant fire. We weren't safe here; boats, motors, monitoring equipment would all perish in short order. There was a cabin journal on the table, signed by the canoeists who had paddled the Seal River over the past ten years, and probably the most irreplaceable item there. I grabbed it on my way out the door. The fire was catching up to us; I could feel the hot breath of it, the smell of it, and the pervasive tension caught us up once again as we climbed into our canoes.

Leaning on our paddles, we distanced ourselves from the fire, covering another eight kilometres before we felt that it was safe enough to pitch camp. All of us were white-faced and exhausted. Clear of the smoke, which now painted an ominous scene to the western horizon, looking strangely like a nuclear oblation, we realized that we were finally outside the gauntlet of wildfires that seemed to be consuming all of Manitoba's northern boreal forests. Perils that still lay ahead, like "Deadly Rapids," and "Deaf Rapids," polar bears, and the run down the Hudson Bay coast would now seem anti-climactic in comparison to what we'd been through already … or so I thought at the time.

I was to guide a writer and photographer from *Men's Journal* magazine on a classic Canadian wilderness canoe trip for a feature story to be published in the spring of 1995. The magazine was the most recent published by *Rolling Stone* out of New York City and the editor wanted the river article to appeal to the new genre of amateur outdoor enthusiasts … the executive jocks with their BMWs, six-figure incomes, and cottages up in the Adirondacks. I envisioned myself wearing a tuxedo while serving Arctic grayling on the lid of my wannigan.

Hodding Carter, writer and part-time postmaster from Thermond, West Virginia, and Russell Kaye, a downtown Brooklyn photographer, had no canoeing experience whatsoever. My assistant, Andy Peppal, was a canoe guide from Camp Keewaydin in Temagami. Andy had problems — serious social-dysfunctional problems as it turned out; but as a favour to his brother, and because Andy had participated in the environmental movement to save Temagami's old-growth forest, I had offered him a guiding job. All this added to the complexity of the trip. I worried more about Andy than having to train neophyte paddlers; I was used to introducing novice adventurers to serious whitewater, but Andy remained a loose cannon. He was a stoner, a sociopath ... but my peers had pleaded with me to take him along, dry him out a bit, give him some responsibility.

Manitoba's Seal River would be the assigned trip. It was the province's wildest river. Unlike the Nelson and the Churchill, which had been dammed for hydropower, the Seal remained unscathed, virtually untrammelled and pristine. The Seal rises at Tadoule Lake, a thousand kilometres north of Winnipeg, and flows through a road-less wilderness to Hudson Bay. The upper reach flows through boreal forest and sand eskers, through the Big Spruce River Delta, and accelerates into dramatic rapids at the gorges at Great Island. Traversing the "Land of Little Sticks" or the transitional boreal treeline, the lower reach flows through subarctic tundra. Boulder fields and wide, complex rapids terminate in a broad estuary at Hudson Bay, forty-five kilometres north of Churchill. The Chipwyan, or Sayisi Dene People, lived in the small community of Tadoule, with a population of 250; it is the only settlement for two hundred kilometres.

Canada Parks had also contributed to the expedition which would help initiate a comprehensive river survey that would last four years and cover over 3,500 kilometres and nineteen wild rivers. The Seal was indoctrinated into the Heritage River System in 1992, for natural heritage values, including its boreal/arctic transitional ecosystem, glacial and river processes, and wildlife. Freshwater seals were abundant and travelled as far as two hundred kilometres upriver, while polar bears ranged the coastline of Hudson Bay. The estuary of the Seal held the highest concentration of beluga whales in the world. The Seal had it all, from human heritage and archaeological potential, to outstanding wilderness recreational attributes. Only a handful of people descend the Seal each year.

Andy and I met Hodding and Russell in Thompson, our start point. Only Andy had been out most of the "packing" day drinking Finesse hairspray with the local bottle suckers in behind the legion. Andy temporarily shaped up after a stern shake down, and we met with a local Chipwyan guide, Tom Ellis, at the Burntwood Diner in downtown Thompson. Tom was a fountain of knowledge about the cultural features along the Seal, but he was concerned about our intentions of sailing down the coast of Hudson Bay to Churchill. "Don't cross Button Bay," Tom warned. "People have died trying; *Tu Cho* (Dene word for "Big Water" or Hudson Bay) is too powerful."

It was tempting, Tom had told us, to cross the twenty-kilometre Button Bay instead of following the coast around to Churchill. We were well-equipped to do the trip, even to sail down the coast if we lashed the canoes; but we also had the option to get Jackie Bastone to pick us up in his Bay boat at the Seal estuary.

"Watch the polar bears at the coast," Tom added. "The rangers tag the bears that drift into Churchill, the bad ones, and fly them out and drop them off at the Seal."

Something else to worry about.

We boarded Skyward Aviation's "Bandit," a twin-engine E-110 Bandeirante. It would take just over an hour to make the three-hundred-kilometre trip north to the Dene village of Tadoule. Once in the air, we could immediately see the smoke haze from at least a dozen wildfires burning — all out of control. If the smoke gets bad enough, the government will evacuate a reserve, elders and children first, as they were now doing at North Indian Lake, and as they would do in two days time at Tadoule while we were there. The burnt spruce smell clung to our nostrils as the Bandit pitched through a wall of smoke against a strong northeast headwind. I felt like throwing up.

I looked out the window and tried to concentrate on the land and lakescape below. It resembled a mosaic puzzle of sand eskers and patches of spruce and fenland interspersed with the lakes that comprised at least half of the puzzle. We had entered the northwestern boreal uplands region of Manitoba where the land was in a state of transition between the boreal forest and the arctic tundra, a bio-region that extends far into the Northwest Territories and envelops sections of the Coppermine, Thelon, Kazan, and Dubawnt rivers — Land of Little Sticks — Canada's Subarctic.

It seemed that most of the town of Tadoule came out to greet the plane. In all-terrain vehicles and battered pickup trucks they descended on the airport, vying to get a job transporting our gear down to the waterfront, a kilometre away.

We met up with filmmaker Alan Code and his wife, Mary (a Dene Native), who together had recently produced a video about the Seal and the Sayisi Dene history. Long before white European imperialist influence, the Edthen-El-Deli Dene, the most eastern of the Dene People, or "caribou-eaters" (an ethnological/anthropological label; the Sayisi Dene prefer to be known as "the People Under the Sun"), travelled the barren grounds along the ribbon-like eskers, following the caribou migrations. The great caribou herds have since changed their travel patterns, much to the dismay of the Sayisi Dene. Some believe it was the interference by mining prospectors and activity close to the river crossings in the fifties and sixties, or government caribou tagging surveys carried out at the same time that precipitated the change. Whites blame the Dene, along with the Inuit people, for overhunting, killing thousands of caribou and not stopping the hunt until they ran out of bullets. The Dene believed that the caribou "belonged" to them and any mass slaughter was vindicated by years of hardship and starvation endured by the people. The caribou hunt took precedence over the fur trade, much to the chagrin of HBC factors at Fort Prince of Wales in Churchill, who had trouble conscripting the Dene as trappers.

The government finally herded the Dene together in the 1960s and forced them to live in a shack town near the Churchill dump. It corresponded with the period of prospecting taking place along the Seal watershed; with them removed from the scene, mining companies didn't have to worry about potential conflicts that may arise from their activities near caribou runs.

But without connection to the land, ostracized by the whites in Churchill, and left to fend for themselves, the Dene people almost slipped into oblivion. Wracked by poverty, abuse, and suicide, the elders made a motion to move back to their homeland of their own volition, without compensation or support from the Manitoba or federal government. The new village was built on an esker at the northeast end of Tadoule Lake, a string of plywood and board dwellings strung out with no particular pattern to the village.

The Dene are a fiercely proud people with close ties to the land around them. The men still engage in traditional "hand games" and talk about the old days, the caribou hunt, and of battles with their enemies, the Inuit and the Cree. The paltry few canoeists who paddle the Seal usually spend little time at the village, choosing to move their gear and canoes down to the lake as quickly as they can. The Dene are gregarious, if given the chance, and enjoy talking with outsiders — except once, perhaps, when an elder followed a couple of kayakers to the lake and placed a curse on them, thinking they were Inuit enemies.

Alan had invited us to stay a few days and partake in a traditional ceremony performed by three visiting Navajo healers. The Navajo and Dene have anthropological roots, sharing the same language and beliefs even though they live thousands of kilometres apart. Hodding and I helped cut and peel twenty-foot spruce poles to be used in the sweat lodge ceremony. Unfortunately, at that time the government was evacuating elders and children because of the fire, now only two kilometres away. Ceremonies were postponed but I did manage to persuade the Navajo healers into giving us a private one instead.

Hodding and I were able to track down the Navajo healers who were staying in the village guest house near the lake. Russell and Andy had wandered off along the esker to the north to see how close the fire was to the village. It was dusk by this time and no light was coming from the shack, except for the incident glow from a TV accompanied by the sound of laughter. The three healers had been watching a movie, *Robin Hood: Men in Tights*, and eating a late dinner of microwave entrees. The TV was quickly turned off when they saw us at their door.

A couple of packages of Borkum Riff tobacco and fifty dollars cash weren't enough to buy us a couple of buttons of peyote, but it was sufficient to procure a water ceremony. The Navajo men cleared the floor and set

151

down a beautifully ornate wooden box. It contained the healer's religious items; eagle feathers, various smudges, polished stones, and ornamental bones were laid out in front of the eldest of the three Natives. He handed Hodding a Styrofoam cup and asked him to go to the lake and bring it back filled with water. When he returned, the shaman was already chanting and waving the smoke smudge around the room. Hodding and I sat cross-legged, watching and listening while the Navajo blessed the water in the cup. He blew smoke into the container and said something in Chipwyan then handed Hodding the vessel.

"Drink a quarter of this," the healer said. After Hodding was finished, I drank a quarter cup and set it down on the floor.

"Take the cup and make sure your friends drink the water," the Navajo elder told us. We left carrying half a cup of blessed water, looking for Russell and Andy. By the time we found Russell, who had been out photographing a hand-game at the community centre, there was only a mouthful of water left in the cup. Andy had disappeared. Russell was glad to have had the ceremonial water; the angst and uncertainty of travelling in the Canadian wilderness was helping him to establish a more spiritual footing. A fourth member of our party had been left out and I hoped that it wasn't earmarking some kind of future dilemma or incident.

Alan had told us that the private ceremony was a good idea. It also showed the Dene our respect for both their culture and the power of the river — a custom I learned to accept with devout seriousness over the years. The Seal is a complex waterway with many dangers, and we knew we would be heading into Manitoba's worst wildfires. For me the trip was particularly unnerving — I would later learn that Andy had managed to pimp some dope from the Dene police constable, and later when the going got tough, Andy would get stoned.

It was a 385-kilometre paddle from Tadoule to Churchill, with an elevation drop of nearly three hundred metres. Eighty percent of the forty-two rapids would be technical runs, some over ten kilometres long, with a variable current of five to fifteen kilometres per hour. We were heavily loaded: three weeks of provisions, "traditional" gear including two wannigans and a reflector oven, and close to seventy-five kilograms of photography equipment Russell had brought along.

The seventeen-foot canoes were rigged with detachable spray covers; these would be indispensable on the bigger rapids or if we chose to sail down the Hudson Bay coast. Because of the steady current and voluminous rapids, most Seal River adventurers have been using motored rafts and not canoes.

Unlike Canadian Shield rivers to the south, the Seal's water flow peaks in June instead of April or May, and recedes quickly after that, generally exposing shallow, bouldery rapids. The prevailing wind is also out of the north and east, making travel down the Bay coast particularly hazardous. Alan also warned us not to cross Button Bay as we pushed off from Tadoule against a stiff southeast wind. It was early July. The water was cold … the lake ice having just melted off. The wind had an Arctic edge to it and whipped against our faces for three days, eventually forcing us to lie up on Negassa Lake after being pushed back by metre-high waves. We were forced to pitch camp on a tiny beach in a recent burn. The only wind protection was the shelter we made of an overturned canoe and a rain fly. But it was sufficient enough to keep a fire going, eat fresh-caught lake trout, stay dry, and smoke our pipes.

The river was swollen with winter melt, heaving the rapids into furious standing waves, some over two metres high. Mosquitoes and black flies assaulted us at every moment while not on the water, and during the day there was no respite from the scourge of horseflies that would bite at any exposed flesh whether we were on the water or not. The Dene kids called them "bulldogs" and would eat them as candy. At the village, they showed me how to dislodge the gel-sac by squeezing the abdomen (after pulling off the wings), then licking the sweet bubble of nectar from the carcass. Horseflies are basically nectar-eaters when they aren't sucking the blood of animals.

For Russell, who had never done anything like this before, it was traumatic; assault after assault from all forces of Nature with no reprieve. He was having a tough time of it, mostly because of his inexperience and lack of confidence. Hodding was born with a *joie de vivre* and took everything in stride, complained about nothing, and worked hard at learning the skills. As Russell became adept at paddling strokes and camp chores, he relaxed more into the trip and was able to concentrate on his photography. Andy had gone into his own self-indulgent world; he was no longer an assistant to me, countering any decision I made about route selection, safety considerations, or respect for needs other than his own. He began rooting through the food packs and treating Hodding and Russell to treats that were supposed to be saved only for morale boosters at the end of, or during, hard days of travel; or he would argue about what meals to prepare for dinner, disregarding the strict adherence to the expedition menu. During an expedition, the allotment of food is carefully organized and rationed each day; Andy broke the cardinal rule of guiding by challenging the leader, stealing specialty foods, and disrupting the menu plan.

Andy had already used up his insect repellent and was bumming it off the rest of us. Refusing to wear a protective bug-jacket and just a pair of cut-off shorts, Andy relied on the heavy lathering of DEET-laden bug dope on all his exposed skin. DEET (*N, N-Diethyl-meta-toluamide*) is a harmful chemical absorbed into the bloodstream and has the ability to melt plastic. Prolonged use can cause behavioural problems, poor muscle coordination, neurological disorders, and brain cell death.

During this time, while trying to impress Hodding and Russell with his cavalier presence, Andy's flesh had reacted to too much insect repellent and was breaking out in blisters and running sores. This wasn't enough to dissuade him from over-applying the repellent; however, he did sport the best tan of us all. The rest of us kept covered, either with heavy canvas clothes and bug-jackets, or our wetsuits when we were running whitewater. It was getting increasingly more difficult to abate Andy's actions in front of the others; he used them as a shield and an audience. I didn't want Andy's personality disorder to be the theme of the magazine story, yet he demanded everyone's attention, mostly the curiosity of the clients or through admonishments from me. Andy was the only one who didn't partake in the Dene ceremony at Tadoule.

Samuel Hearne was commissioned by the Hudson's Bay Company out of Fort Prince of Wales (Churchill) to explore the barrenlands in quest of the fabled copper mines that were said to exist "twelve to twenty-four months near a permanently frozen sea." Both his 1769 and 1770 trips were unsuccessful. However, he did spend considerable time camped on Shethanei Lake (with his bevy of young Dene girls to keep him warm) and gave us our first European account of the Seal River. We camped on one of Hearne's wintering sites, adjacent to a glacial hill, while the pall of the distant fires created an eerie glow that was nothing short of supernatural.

There was a deep lagoon or runnel about a hundred metres from our pitched tents, forming a levee between the lake and a bog marsh. Several caribou runs led away from the camp in no particular pattern, and it was soon evident that one could easily get lost trying to follow any one of them. But the most noteworthy geomorphological feature of Hearne's campsite environs was the prominent rock mound that rose at least thirty metres above the treetops and was situated an easy five-minute walk from camp. It was obviously a drumlin of sorts; not the type composed of gravel and clay, but of blocks of granite piled helter skelter, forming hundreds of cave-like hollows and caverns that would be choice enclosures as black bear dens. Some of the rocks were unstable, precariously balanced, requiring some climbing skill and sure-footedness to gain access to the summit and the spectacular view. A scattering of dwarf birch had commanded a foothold in the soil-less environment, testimony of the obstinate and determined nature of the tundra life forms.

It was a rock-hound's Mecca. Literally hundreds of rock types and minerals lay exposed; biotite schists, sandstones, quartz, and conglomerates, both along the beach and all over the drumlinoid hill where we now stood. Minute specs of mica sparkled iridescently in the early evening sun, which had finally cleared itself of the thick strata of cloud that had dominated the sky all day. There was clearly a strong energy here — perhaps a spiritual energy as there often is at these strange places. I was convinced that the striking oddity of this geological structure would have been some type of ceremonial gathering site for the early people.

Andy had brought the skull of a caribou with him to the top of the hill. He had discovered the skeleton along one of the trails behind the campsite. We all agreed that it should stay where we stood and be used for a ceremony later that evening. We found a cleft in the rock where we could all sit out of the wind, and the skull was perched on the highest boulder.

155

The strange band of open, clear sky did not move out of the horizon all that day, contrasted by the weight of a leaden and bleak sheathe of cloud. We had almost forgotten about the fires and wondered whether Allan and the remaining village men had been evacuated. The evenings were deliciously long, and it was hard to stay still, to relax after a hard day's paddle. We were deep into conversation, sitting by the campfire, when the hue of evening light changed abruptly. Andy and Hodding ran to the beach to view the setting sun but Russell and I were already half-way to the drumlin hill, cameras in hand, and my medicine bag over my shoulder.

That's the peculiar thing about nature photography; the incident light is only temporary, fleeting, and always remarkable. Always, there is a moment of hesitation and the difficulty of choosing to see something special through the clarity of your own vision, rather than through the limited scope of a camera lens. With the latter, there is something lost of the magic and also a prevailing sense of urgency to capture the moment on film.

As the sun set across Shethanei Lake, the tops of the spruce trees facing the light glowed brilliant orange, as if suddenly splashed with fire. We couldn't climb the pile of boulders quick enough getting to the top, each rock glowing like a hot coal. But it was just the ambient light of the sun, projected oddly through the haze of smoke over Tadoule, natural, yet amorphous, casting such brilliance over the landscape. It seemed to have a spectral purpose.

Andy and Hodding reached the top moments after we did, and the four of us stood, mouths agape, and looked out over the chromatic sea of spruce, transformed from a monotonous green to crimson splendour. The esker sand ridges across the lake resembled red snakes, uncoiled and peaceful.

For less than half an hour, Shethanei was suspended in colour animation, the intensity ebbing as the sun set just before midnight. We quickly gathered in the depression chosen for our ceremony. I placed some tobacco in the caribou skull cavity, lit a smudge stick of cedar and sage, and wafted the four of us in a liberal cleansing of sweet smoke. Everyone took a caribou tooth for good luck. The homily was simple and heartfelt, and we finished the ceremony by placing the caribou skull on top of the rock again. It was a profound experience, timely, purposeful, and symbolic.

Shethanei Lake to the Dene refers to "the hill going into the lake." A large esker literally disappears into the north shore narrows and reappears on the side of the lake we were camping on. The size of the lake was daunting but we enjoyed an unusual calm for the next three days. The time we spent at Shethanei was an almost surreal experience; the serpentine eskers, golden spires of dune-sand, rose above the spruce veld and would catch the fading rays of the evening sun. The full darkness of a deep summer night, so familiar in southerly regions, was never attained, and the fires raging in the distance created a numinous haze around the sun and permeated the landscape in an illusory glow.

Midnight treks along the eskers afforded an unprecedented look at the surrounding boreal landscape and animal activity, as well as an opportunity to explore the boreal bioregion away from the river. On one occasion I came face to face with a tundra wolf as I stepped over an embankment into a sand blowout (depression on top of an esker). We shared a moment of uncertainty, neither of us moving until I made a motion to unsling my camera. The wolf bolted, paused briefly to look back at me, and then disappeared.

Pioneer lichens and mosses grew over the eskers in circular and polygonal mosaic designs in a struggle to stabilize the eroding dunes, while scattered clumps of dwarf birch and jack pine clung to the edges of the sand world with a fierce tenacity, subject to the almost incessant winds and interminably long winters. The vista from the eskers offered an unrestricted view over the endless plain of black spruce and tundra bog.

One of our campsites had a park-like landscape with a long, low esker snaking inland away from the lake. Copses of birch trees decorated an almost golf-course-like tended lawn. After abandoning the eskers as a travelway, this was a place where the Dene would come in the summer to cut birch bark for their canoes. Beneath a large spruce, partly protected from the elements, was a neatly stacked pile of birchbark rolls, obviously intended to be picked up at some time by Native canoe builders. It was either forgotten or purposely left behind nearly a century ago.

It was a 240-kilometre paddle to the Bay from Shethanei, dropping seven hundred vertical feet in a long series of steep-pitched rapids. We stopped briefly at the junction of the Wolverine River ("Nah yah eye desay" to the Dene, or "River that drains soaked-through Lake"), and we caught our first Arctic grayling at the foot of the rapids. It was here also that we spotted our first harbour seals playing near some centre channel boulders, eyeing us curiously, or sunning themselves on the rocks, blending inconspicuously against the grey of the stone.

Fires were looming downriver and it was decided that we'd stop at the base of a thirty-metre-high esker and pitch camp. From the apex of the dune I could get a protracted view of where the fire was spreading, plot its movement on the topo map, and chart which direction the smoke was blowing. Since leaving Shethanei Lake we had been following the sheer-line of smoke, managing to keep it out of our faces by less than half a kilometre. Tomorrow could be different; the fire was following the south shore of the river and if the wind came up, the possibility of it jumping to the opposite side was likely — if that happened we would either have to hold up or try to get in front of the inferno. It was the smoke we were worried more about than the actual fire.

It had been unseasonably hot the past few days, in marked contrast to the first three on leaving Tadoule. That evening we feasted on grayling and fresh-baked cornbread, under the shadow of the esker behind us and the auspicious cloud of smoke downriver. I had knots in my stomach and tried to weed them out by walking the crest of the esker alone while the others sat at the camp. Everyone was getting along, and for now Andy seemed to have straightened out, at least enough so that I didn't have to keep such a watchful eye on him, and he would follow my lead closely while running rapids, or carry out chores on his own without me grilling him.

I walked for several kilometres. It was easy going and my legs seemed to flex on their own, one step at a time, mind racing, thinking about the past week, what lay ahead, and how crazy this whole adventure was. The esker trailed off to the north, a natural trail that was not hard to follow without actually paying much attention; that was the lure of it — you were drawn onward by the simplicity of it, away from the river noise, the promising quiet, the aloneness. Like any trail, you were compelled to follow it to the end; but here it seemed to go on forever. If it ended, it just retreated into the landscape temporarily, and you could see it surfacing a short distance away, the yellowed back of a sand serpent. Twilight added to the spell, and there was no rush to get back, to beat the waning sun and expected darkness. There were wolf dens dug into the side of esker mounds, the history of meals displayed in a variety of bone fragments covering the entrance path. There were grave sites with weathered pickets bleached grey by sun and pitted by weather, scattered about, the dead now long forgotten, and places where animal bones mingled with those of humans ... life and death along the trail.

In the morning, we didn't have to paddle very far before getting a good view of the fire burning along the river's edge. With the current pulling at ten kilometres per hour, interspersed with long sets of rapids, we had little chance of backtracking if the fire and smoke proved to be intolerable. We had played our cards, or rather I had dealt out everyone's hand because I held the deck, betting that the winds had forced the smoke to rise vertically — and it did — instead of hanging in a deadly shroud over the Seal.

At one point we stopped along the shore at the head of the blaze in order to get some photographs, but the intense heat seared our bare skin and showers of glowing sparks and airborne cinders fell like rain on top of the canoes, forcing us to retreat further down the river. Each dry spruce at the leading edge of the fire would literally explode into a ball of fire, sending a plume of black smoke skyward, adding to the conflagration — an entity that moved with the sole purpose of destroying whatever lay in its path. At least it was safer to stay out toward the centre of the river, away from the flames and the heat, playing the rapids cautiously as we rounded river bends not knowing what waited for us ahead.

We ran twelve sets of rapids over forty-five kilometres that day, often shooting difficult runs while the forest on both sides of the river was fully ablaze. We were in a broiler, being turned and slow-cooked in a fluvial convection oven. Adrenalin ran as high as the smoke-cloud; we were fearful always of the unpredictable nature of our situation, running on nervous energy and good luck. And at some point of the day we managed to outrun the fires and made camp on a beautiful beach at the west end of Great Island (or *Nu Cho* meaning "big island") — a hundred-metre rise in elevation where the Seal splits into two distinct channels. This was a spiritual place for the Sayisi Dene, where certain rocks were once collected for medicinal healing purposes.

It was the narrowest section of the Seal River, and the fire burned close to the campsite throughout the night, somewhat subdued by the cool and damp air. If the wind had changed direction, the fire would have easily "jumped" the river, to our side, necessitating a quick departure off the beach. It was decided that we would rest over a day to let the fire pass through and hike the nearby esker that overlooks the North Channel. Someone had erected a monument on the esker for the late Bill Mason, filmmaker and icon paddler; Bill had never paddled the Seal, nonetheless it was a polite gesture to the Canadian adventurer.

Again, the hike along the esker ridge was alluring, dreamlike and illusory, the golden sand of the esker standing out in marked contrast to the dull greys and greens. The silica in the sand seemed to attract and absorb the waning sunlight and hold the hue deep into the growing shadows of the subarctic midnight. Distant fires glowed and smouldered all around us but the air over the esker was fresh and summery warm. A bull moose glided across a depression below us, huffing and panting, seemingly moving on a cushion of air, graceful for such a large animal. It was nearly one in the morning by the time we returned to the campsite.

The fire had completely gutted "Bastion Rock," a vertical fortress of rock circled by one calm channel and a rather energetic class 4 rapid through the main channel. We made early camp here as the fires were not far downriver. Tents were pitched over recently scorched earth and it wasn't unusual to find the bones of incinerated animals that had no place to escape to. Known for its density of cliff swallows, there were no birds to be seen or heard — just the onrush of the rapids. The main fire had jumped the river here, passed through, and was now burning about a kilometre away. Holding up at Bastion Rock for the afternoon was a good idea, just to let the fire and smoke distance itself. From a rise I could see a wall of smoke moving off downriver, toward one of the toughest rapids on the Seal.

Nine Bar Rapids normally required a carry-over portage around a ledge that ran across the entire river. Every northern river has one iconic rapid that stands out, is generally feared or approached with caution, and run carefully — or not at all. Nine Bar is just such a rapid, and it demanded our closest attention. We beached the canoes in an eddy at the approach of the whitewater. The hydraulic pull of the river was fierce, angry, seething with layer upon layer of white, turbulent water as far as we could see. Even the river here seemed to be running away from something, racing to the Arctic sea, whipped into a frenzy by some greater entity. Lunch sat on my stomach in a coagulated lump. I managed to get a partial view of about half the rapids from a low rise behind our lunch station. The river was about half a kilometre wide at this point, wider than most other rapids which were deep and fast. Here, the river ran shallow and fast with an extraordinary vertical drop, producing a technical nightmare for safe running. The only way down was to play the rapids nearer the shore so we could pull out and scout ahead. But it's never easy to scout a rapid like this as it always shape-shifts into something else once you get in the thick of it, and then you forget your best intentions. You just go for it and play each boulder that looms in front of you, avoid the sucking ledges and whirlpools, always looking beyond to see if you're not orchestrating a disaster by working the wrong channel.

It never works out the way you want it to. Sometimes you just get lucky. We worked the rapid for about one-third of the way, stopped, and scouted to see if we could see the infamous ledge; but the water ran high and everything looked the same. If the water was lower, the ledge would be clearly defined, and it wasn't. Pushing off for the second time we played it too far to the centre of the run, lessening our chances of pulling off to scout. We were now committed to the rapids in its entirety, the ledge now appearing as a broad sheerline drop that traversed the entire river — an optical illusion from above, like a hologram that concealed a very different picture if you looked at it from another perspective.

Andy's canoe was to my right and behind. I was waving my paddle at him to get over more to river right as there was a narrow sluiceway of smooth water over the two-metre ledge. I yelled at Russell to back-paddle to give us more time to line up. The other canoe made it through but we were still too far to the left.

"Paddle as hard as you can," I yelled at Russell.

"Brace over the ledge than power forward and give it all you got!"

There was no way we could have made it to the smooth tongue over the ledge; instead we lined up the canoe for an almost vertical drop into a hydraulic pool. Known as a souse-hole or "keeper," these were dangerous at any time, usually filled with aerated water with little buoyant properties, pulling everything that enters it back into the fall of water, over and over again.

There was no time for discussion, no time to acknowledge your own fear; any hesitation would kill us both. If we overturned in the keeper there would be no rescue. Not while we were alive, anyway. Even with our wetsuits on, the cold water would kill us in less than thirty minutes, if we didn't drown first trying to extricate ourselves from the hole. Even with that, the escape down the rapids would be a long float on your back and the likelihood that hypothermia would set in before you could reach shore. And if you did manage to do it, you would then have to get a fire going, somehow, while your extremities hung limp and useless. There was no firewood here, and the shoreline was thick with willow and wiry sedge. But death wasn't an option.

Russell literally disappeared when the bow of the canoe went over and hit the bottom pool. A huge wave rolled back over the deck of the canoe and hit me in the face, nearly knocking the paddle out of my hand. The canoe remained dangerously stationary for a moment, drifting back slowly toward the hydraulic fall. We nearly lost it. At this point the river was mostly air and the boat listed from one side to the other as we tried for purchase with our paddles, scooping little more than river foam.

"Paddle harder," I yelled at Russell, knowing that he couldn't have put much more into his strokes. I edged the canoe over to the sheerline of water, steering toward the outer edge of the hole where the river flowed downstream. It was our only way out. When we hit it, the canoe was lifted half into the air, exiting the hydraulic pool with a rush and heading downstream on a rollercoaster ride finish.

Luckily, as it turned out, because any hesitation or upset in the rapids would have put us directly in, or behind, the most frightening of all the fires encountered so far. Nine Bar was run in its entirety, including the two-metre drop over the ledge. Energy spent, we pulled over to the shore near the bottom of the rapids to rest. Andy went to take a piss. That's when Hodding started screaming about the fire. There was no rest. Death was still at the back door; we paddled for our lives amidst a shower of soot and burning embers.

For over a hundred kilometres, the fires burned along the Seal, and we were never actually clear of the smoke at any time during our trip. Even as we neared the Bay coast and drifting into the open, treeless tundra, the smoke shroud was always there, as portentous as distant thunderheads in the horizon.

Past Great Island, Nine Bar, and the retreat from the water-monitoring station (where the fire actually terminated but destroyed the camp), we entered a new bioregion of treeless heath and peat plateaus. The river dropped steadily through long rapids and boulder trains known as *felsenmeer* or "rock meadows." The transitional boreal forest was behind us, replaced by scabrous tufts of black spruce and wide expanses of tundra heath. At the last campsite before Hudson Bay, I cut poles for a sailing rig to be used to make the canoes more seaworthy for the coast run. The smoke haze was still a part of the surface landscape; the sunlight was filtered through the fire effluent, transforming the earth and air into an ochrous panorama.

In the morning, while twenty kilometres west of our last rapids, we lashed the canoes together and hoisted the sail to give it a test run. With the wind behind us, we managed to manoeuvre the canoes through the final several sets of rapids under sail. It was an interesting and demanding change in skill tactic, having to line up a virtual sailing craft to run boulder-garden rapids, ledge drops, and to facilitate eddy-turns and cross-ferries as one would normally do with only one canoe. The current was strong and the estuary of the Seal broke off into multiple channels, making it difficult to select which way to go. Taking the wrong channel could have led us into a rock hell with little hope of backtracking upriver against the high water rush.

Fog can obscure Deaf Rapids — "deaf" because the paddler cannot hear or see the rapid from the above approach even on a clear day. The pitch was severe, dropping over fifty feet in less than half a kilometre. From the head of the rapids we could see Hudson Bay, but the last half of the rapids remained obscured. We disassembled the canoes, packing the spruce poles in the bottom of the boats so we wouldn't lose them, even if we dumped in the rapids. There was no way to line the canoes along the shore because of the thick willow and high water. Most canoeists opt to carry their boats around the rapids — a tough bush-push through willow thickets and boulder gardens. We were determined to complete the Seal without having to make one single portage.

The centre of Deaf Rapids was un-runnable; the rollers would easily flip even a much larger vessel, let alone a small craft like a canoe. We chose to run the class 3 left side and take our chances with the large boulders that projected out into the river. Both canoes made it down without incident. The tide was going out, turning the last couple of kilometres into a staircase of ledges. We had to backtrack when we realized we had gone too far; we were in the coastal zone and needed to find a place to camp until the next high tide. Originally, we were to head for Jackie Bastone's goose camp up the coast which would have afforded us some protection from bears, but it could only be reached at high tide. We were stuck where we were.

The coast itself was not a clear line, but an endless field of large boulders, gravel bars and islands tufted with course willow … and there was the threat of polar bears that ranged the estuary in search of beached beluga whales and seals. The bugs were so thick we had to pitch our tent on a small island, amongst the sedge, with no clear line of sight in case a bear approached. We ate dinner in the tent. Silence. Exhaustion. The race down the river of fire took its toll on us all. I pulled a couple of large cans of Sapporo beer out of a barrel-pack that I had hidden away until this moment and we drank them with raised spirits. I duct-taped my flashlight onto the shotgun and loaded the slugs instead of the Bear Scare. Any confrontation would be sudden, with no time to change clips — Bear Scare wouldn't be effective at close range.

The coastline lay ahead of us. Others had tried it; some turned back, some arranged for boat pickup, while others had even perished in the violent storms that ripped across Hudson Bay. When you travel the coast you are entirely at the mercy of the winds. And when they hit, the coast is not a hospitable place to be, offering little in the way of protection.

We slept uneasily, taking turns to keep a vigilant watch during the half-light of night. The tide came in around 11:00 a.m. the next morning. With the canoes once again rigged for sailing, we pushed off into the calm waters of the estuary, passing about two dozen harbour seals before reaching the expanse of the Bay. About two hundred metres out from the last of the shore boulders, we encountered our first beluga whales. We heard them first, blowing air and water, and the sonar-like sounds of their voices, otherworldly and enchanting. White ghosts appeared, dozens of them, all around the canoes. Some passed within a metre underneath the boats, looking up with supernatural eyes, barely rippling the surface of the water. Gentle, curious beings, some with young attached to their backs, surfacing and submarining only feet away from us. Hard to believe that they were almost exterminated, killed for their oil and meat, these affable spirits of Tu Cho.

We had a six-hour run down the coast before the next low tide. Soon we would be beached on the flats and boulder plains of mud and sand for as far as the eye could see. A Spielberg setting. A crude sailing vessel dwarfed by the expansive tideland, the smoke-filled sky creating a strange ambiance in the twilight. We had six more hours to wait for the next high tide, hopefully remaining windless so that we didn't have to retreat for cover along the coast — the phantom coast that shape-shifts with the tide and remains invisible and elusive. It came in after midnight, much more quickly, in fact, than it had gone out. We were once again afloat with a light breeze to carry us down the coast. I tied my candle lantern to the mast, more to shed a friendly glow over the canoes than to be effective at anything else. In a way, it helped dispel some of the nervousness about making a midnight run. My compass, at this point, was invaluable to keep us on course; GPS was not yet on the commercial market. There were no land bearings in the dark, except for the occasional boulder we would get hung up on temporarily, spin around, readjust with the wind and direction, and sail on knowing we were still within a kilometre of the coastline. Then things got a little crazy.

Andy insisted we paddle across Button Bay. The first lights from Churchill began showing dimly, twenty kilometres to the east, eerily floating on the horizon, fading in and out of view. We had been warned not to cross over, to stay with the coast all the way and resist the temptation to make the shortcut. Hodding, Russell, and I were in agreement but Andy persisted, chastising us for our timidity. It was Andy's turn to steer the canoes while we slept. I told him to keep the course down the coast. He didn't answer.

I was dreaming; deep, lucid waves of emotion, people, events passing through my unconscious mind. I was exhausted and had slept uneasily for several nights, and Andy was up to his old tricks. When sleep came it was from fatigue; I had wasted a lot of energy on mitigating the effect of Andy's actions on the dynamic of the expedition. We were all tired of his foolishness. It was the rocking of the boats and the spray of water that woke me up. The sail was full and we were running strong with the offshore breeze … *straight across Button Bay toward Churchill!* The canoes were held together with two spruce poles barely the width of my wrist and they were now straining hard under the surge of waves that now pummelled the bow. I told Andy to let up on the rudder and turn the canoes back to shore. He ignored me and leaned on his paddle even more. Russell and Hodding were terrified, shouting at me to do something. I yelled at Andy again. No response. It was getting rougher and I knew the boats wouldn't hold up for the crossing.

"Pull the sail down," I yelled at the bowsmen. Hodding and Russell wrestled with the tarp sail and the lines holding it taut and managed to get it down. I pushed back the spray-cover and exposed the gun case so Andy could see. I started to pull the rifle out of its sheath with the intent to shoot the man beside me if he didn't let up on the steering course. Andy threw down his paddle. "It's your boat!" he said angrily, crossing his arms and refusing to help paddle the canoes back the three kilometres to the coastal course and calm water. It was a scene out of the movie *The Caine Mutiny*, only it wasn't a movie, it was really happening. The thought of nearly having to kill someone sickened me; I just wanted the trip to be over, and to distance myself from this insane man.

As daylight emerged we found ourselves at the bottom of Button Bay, ready to sail the last twenty kilometres to Churchill. We had passed several large pods of belugas, swimming in formation or cruising at us from one side or the other, often passing under the boats so closely I could reach down and touch them. The trip wasn't officially over until we moored the canoes beside an old tug tied up alongside the kilometre-long grain elevator loading dock, stepped ashore on solid ground, walked into town, and had a cold beer and a greasy hamburger. Andy headed for the local bar to bum cigarettes.

Hodding had his story; his first draft being turned down as a novelette instead of a feature, it took him two years to whittle down something *Men's Journal* could actually print. Hodding and I had our photographs which would find outlets in magazines around the world. As for Andy, we had half the town of Churchill looking for him when the train was ready to leave for Thompson. He had our tickets. Someone found him drinking beer at the legion, oblivious that the train was held up because of him. Andy couldn't understand why nobody wanted to talk with him on the long train ride home. Everyone sat alone.

Two hours into the train ride, Russell came and sat down beside me. For a while he said nothing, and then he turned to me and we talked openly about the expedition for the first time. When the magazine had asked him to go, Russell had told them that he couldn't refuse. They had agreed to outfit and pay him handsomely for the photography. Russell said that the more he learned about the river, the less he liked the idea of going, regardless of the remuneration. He had been afraid, in over his head. Initially, he had thought nothing of the risks involved. He figured that if the guides had their shit together and he was supplied with a lifejacket, things would be okay. Back in Thompson, when Andy showed up in the hotel bar zonked on Finesse hair-spray, it was a slap in the face of reality. Russell admitted that his most profound experience of the trip was his own naivety about risk-taking, calculating his chances of survival, and accepting decisions as possibly the last ones he would ever make. His greatest fear, other than dying, was being a burden on the group.

We shook hands for a long time, slow and deliberate; he thanked me for getting him out alive, and I assured him that it was mostly his own resources and willpower that pulled him through. Russell handed me a postcard he had picked up in Churchill, shoved it into my hand and walked away. He was crying. I turned the card over, dated July 20, 1994. It read:

> Hap — It's quite odd to spend that much time with someone you don't really know, fifteen or so feet behind you, feeling their force, their rhythm; almost their breath. We didn't chat much but somehow that's even more of a bond — the quiet, interrupted by that vibrant rumble, shared. Learning to trust that eloquent guidance, I am so warmly indebted. I would enjoy crossing paddles again … and again … Russell

It felt as if a heavy shroud had been lifted from my soul, a grey mist that burns away magically with the morning sun. And as I looked out the window of the train at the monotony of spruce tracing a ragged edge across the horizon, I knew I would come back again, to this wretched and silent place in the Land of Little Sticks.

But adventure is like that — a mix of hard and soft, cruel and timid, promise and disappointment. And it isn't always the trail, or the river, or the landscape that defines a journey. The Seal River is a place of magic, and of a special people who still have their hearts deeply embedded in the golden sands of Sheth tie eye tuay. As for fire, it is the most unpredictable of all the forces of Nature. It is something you cannot plan for or predict. The character of fire demonstrates its control over all living things and the other elements: it creates its own wind and fills the air with its smoky breath; it consumes the landscape and covers the water in an oily patina of ash. Fire teaches us expansion and illumination of the spirit, rejuvenation of the physical properties of existence, and provides the primal gifts of light and warmth. Fire destroys, but it also resurrects and revitalizes a forest. Within its consuming and terrible force there is also a spirituality and purpose. We saw it first-hand. It was a trip of extremes, in both environmental conditions and human interaction; but always, no matter the degree of risk or inherent difficulty, the journey traces a path through the pages of your own life and destiny. Good or bad, it is still a journey.

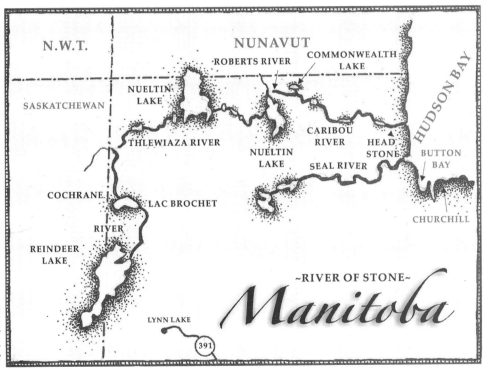

Tundra headstone and Dene waymarker, northern Manitoba.

FIFTEEN
RIVER OF STONE

When a man has not a good reason for doing a thing, he has one good reason for letting it alone.
— Sir Walter Scott

Well, what does a maudlin old minstrel know about the Call of the Wild? There was reason enough, I guess, beyond placating my own whims and pleasures. It wasn't like I was a mountain climber with a death lust where the trail unfolded to my own selfish desires alone. There *was* the lure of the ultimate challenge; there *was* the curiosity of travelling an unknown wilderness. A new trail.

I rolled over in the bunk and tried to sleep. The wind found every crack in the loose window frames to play its solemn music — more like a funeral dirge than a harmony of angels. The tiny plywood shack sat on the edge of the world and shook and trembled as the wind coursed across the tundra flats, relentless in purpose. It was always windy … it never seemed to let up, not for an instant. Polar bears had ravaged the goose camp, broken down the door, pulled out the insulation from the walls, and eaten all the provisions — provisions that were supposed to feed my canoe party of eight tired adventurers. The food was all gone, or perhaps there wasn't much in the way of provisions to begin with. It was a tough expedition and I had prepared and delivered extra rations en route with the expectation that the outfitter had lived up to his promise: when we arrived on the Hudson Bay coast, the goose camp would be well-stocked with supplies. It wasn't. It was in shambles. In fact, the outfitter hadn't even been to his outpost camp in years. The outfitter had lied to me.

Luckily, when we arrived at the shack the wind had let up and the outfitter had landed his plane, only because he had hoped to get us out before the coming storms. He also realized that he was negligent about the well-stocked camp and decided to come in a day earlier, chancing that we had arrived on time.

He took four people back to Churchill and left four of us at the camp. He said he would try to get back and pick us up. That was yesterday. We pooled what food was left in the packs; a bit of *gorp* (good old raisins and peanuts), two tins of sardines, and a bit of flour. The bears had left us a small jar of soup powder. It was a veritable feast. "Wavies," or snow geese, flew over the camp in steady procession, and it was decided that if we had to spend another day in isolation, without provisions, we would use the shotgun to bring a few birds to the table. But we didn't eat. Everyone was so exhausted all we wanted to do was sleep. And I remember having the most wonderful of all sleeps, in that tiny plywood shack that could barely keep out the rain and wind. When the plane arrived I was almost disappointed.

Forty-two days earlier, four of us — two Swiss lads in their twenties, Jori and Walter, and my now ex-wife Stephanie, boarded a DHC-6 twin-engine Otter based at Lynn Lake, Manitoba, and headed for the small village of Brochet at the north end of Reindeer Lake. The Otter cruised at 115 knots, taking less than an hour to arrive at our departure point on the Cochrane River.

Jori and Walter had paddled the Bloodvein with me a couple of years earlier and were able and willing to endure the rigours of such a long trip. There were several misgivings about undertaking a trip across the barrens of northern Manitoba: the sheer length of it, the perceived hardship, lack of usable field information, and a limited time frame amounted to just the incidental reasons. Cliff Jacobsen, a well-known outdoor writer and friend from Minnesota, kindly supplied me with an article he had written two years previous to my trip that outlined the last part of my route along the Caribou River. He called the Caribou River the "River from Hell," intoning doom and gloom from frozen headwater (in July), to rapids too wild to run and impossible to line along with shoreways choked with willow.

Not to be easily dissuaded, I continued to research the entire route, coming up with scant, outdated information — my route was sketchy at best. Real Berard, who produced a prolific set of canoe maps for the Manitoba government in the early 1970s, had left gaping holes in the information trail along this nine-hundred-kilometre route. Although depicted with an artistic charm, any usable map data was of little help. To complete the *Wild Rivers of Manitoba* guidebook project I needed a representative route through the wildest region of the province. The warnings against paddling this route only ignited a deeper passion to explore it. This would be my last trip after four years charting rivers in the province; a long haul on a tight budget, running client trips to make up for the lack of government funding to complete the necessary research.

As a wilderness guide I was doing the unthinkable — taking neophytes and casual paddlers on some of the wildest rivers in the country, rivers I had not previously run expeditions on. It was all new to me, and my clients understood this; in fact, it was one of the attractions of the trip for them — *not* knowing what was around each bend in the river. For me it demanded more concentration on detailed map work, rapid scouting, and timing. Timing would be critical because I was dividing this trip into two parts and I needed to get across the top of the province in time to meet the other half of the group.

The plane dropped us on the Cochrane River, just north of the Dene village of Brochet, close to the Saskatchewan border. Making our way the two hundred kilometres upriver on the Cochrane, we planned to take a series of lakes east to the Thlewiaza River and ride its turbulent waters to Nueltin Lake. From here, we would continue eastward up the East River as far as we could, pond hop southeast to the White Rock River, and downstream to Nejanalini Lake and the Wolverine River. From the Wolverine, we could then portage east across the tundra to the Roberts River which flows into the Caribou. The headwater of the Caribou, at Commonwealth Lake, was five kilometres from the Nunavut border and our rendezvous location with the remaining party. The outfitter had promised us the use of his caribou hunt-shack; he would fly the other members of our group in from Churchill on a prescribed date. From there it was a two-week descent on the Caribou to Hudson Bay. The preciseness of this route was critical. There were precious few rest days built in to the trip and if we fell behind, these "free" days would be eaten up with hard paddling, just to stay on schedule. Rest days were always a valuable commodity; a time to lift spirits, rest, wash clothing, catch up on journal-writing … to do nothing if you preferred.

Once highlighted on the thirty-four 1:50,000 topographical maps, the expedition route looked daunting, and in the end would establish itself as one of the most difficult expeditions in my career as a professional guide and canoeist. It would also be the most inspiring and austere landscape that I may ever hold witness to, although so physically demanding as to defy any accurate description of it.

The Cochrane River bears the name of a surveyor, A.S. Cochrane, who travelled the river in 1881, thirty years after the Hudson's Bay Company erected trade posts at Brochet and Lac Brochet. The North West Company, rival to the HBC, first set up shop in 1795 in an attempt to trade with the Nueltin Lake Dene, who were then trading at Fort Prince of Wales in Churchill. The Chipwyan Dene began filing to the Brochet posts by way of the Robertson Esker — an overland route that followed a series of glacial ridges across the tundra. Once a route had been initiated through the Thlewiaza and Cochrane, most travel eventually took place along this corridor using a combination of overland and river travel trails.

It took us a week to ascend the Cochrane; luckily, the wind favoured our northward trek as we were able to sail upstream for over one hundred kilometres — half the distance to our eastward turnoff point. The many turbulent rapids, however, proved to be quite challenging, requiring lengthy sessions of wading, lining, and vigorous power paddling against the current. The river compromises its directional flow by making an abrupt turn southwest to unite with its headwater lake in Saskatchewan. The entire corridor resides within the Taiga Shield Ecozone, a rolling plain dominated by magnificent rock outcroppings and stunted coniferous forests. The visual landscape covering showed both recent and regenerative scars from forest fire activity, and it was common to see bald eagles and nest sites perched atop dead standing timber along the ridge crests. We camped mostly at what seemed to be traditional Dene hunting sites adjacent to the many eskers along the route and marked by the scattering of bleached caribou bones.

Lac Brochet is a Dene village on the Cochrane, and we stopped there early on in our trip. As we arrived at the dock it seemed as if the whole town took a keen interest in our being there. Children smiled shyly while youths donning Guns & Roses T-shirts were impatient for any news from the south; a strange request as the government's answer to Native social issues was to install the best in multi-channel television reception. But for the young Dene, even though connected by TV and radio to the rest of Canada and the world, they still felt a disconnection by isolation, and our sudden arrival seemed to substantiate, with physical proof, that there was a world beyond theirs. For a brief time, we were the conduit to that other world.

They were joined by teams of adults who, as it turned out, found it quite interesting that we were paddling all the way to Hudson Bay by way of a river that, to them, would take us to Saskatchewan in the other direction. We tried to explain our route to them but few had even travelled that way, except by snowmobile in the winter when they would sometimes hunt around Fort Hall Lake.

At the Band office they were quite honoured that we would take the time to procure the services of a local medicine healer so that we could formally ask permission to travel in Dene Land. They had never seen paddlers before in this part of their country. A ceremony was arranged quickly and I was surprised to meet up with the same guest Navajo healer that I had met in Tadoule on my Seal River trip two years before.

We were taken by pickup to a small house in the centre of the village. Lac Brochet looked as if it had just undergone an overhaul; houses were relatively new and neat and the people well-organized, friendly, and happy. There were far more trucks here than actual kilometres of roads, although the seasonal winter road allowed villagers access to points south, if only for a brief period.

The word had gone out around town that a ceremony was being organized; others joined in and the small house soon became a buzz of excitement. Preparations were made, smudge sticks ignited, and the sweetgrass made its rounds. We were allowed to talk first, as guests, and with that opportunity thanked the Dene for their hospitality and asked permission to travel through their land with humility and respect. All nodded in compliance and then drum beats and wisps of smoke from the smudge carried the enchanting rhythm of the shaman's voice around the room. The ceremony was a hybrid mix of Catholicism and Chipwyan, English and Dene, beautifully delivered, thankfully received. The physical place was abandoned, souls occupied some other dimension, relief and peace prevailed. All trepidation I once felt about the expedition had been neatly exorcised.

The Dene kids were noticeably sad when we paddled off. They followed us down the lake in their own canoes, calling to us, singing and laughing, asking us to come back and stay longer. The young girls flirted with Jori and Walter, teasing them, until their voices faded away behind us.

We left the Cochrane River behind, following caribou trails and paddling a chain of small sapphire-blue lakes divided by small eskers over the height of land. No simple explanation can be made of the distinctive beauty here, a place where we mixed the heavy toil of the portage trail with the pleasing grandeur of pristine landscape. We were leaving any obvious remnants of Precambrian Shield behind, the land now giving precedence to permafrost and thermokarst, heath-rich tundra, polygon peatlands, and discontinuous black spruce parkland that defined the treeline. Although we had not encountered any caribou, their trails were clearly scribed across the tundra: ancient paths perhaps, etched by the great Kaminuriak caribou herds when they used to migrate this far south and west from the Dubawnt and Yathkyed hinterlands. Any mark upon the fragile turf here would last for centuries.

Scads of sun-bleached caribou bones, often mixed with those of humans, were scattered about like pieces of a great terrestrial board game, along game trails and on top of sinewy eskers. Everywhere there was an esker ridge, there were grave sites marked with shards of decayed wooden pickets or small boulders.

Historic Fort Hall was just a forgotten piece of the past. We stood on a high esker looking over Fort Hall Lake, at a narrows before Thanout Lake, the wind picking up considerably since we arrived. It was the 1940 burial site of Petit Casimir, chief of the Barren Land Dene. In order to watch his people pass by in their canoes, it is said that Casimir was consigned to the high esker grave in a standing position. Beside a few weathered bones there was a leather belt with sheathed knife attached, half buried in the esker sand, no doubt one of the chief's prized possessions. Energy here was strong and the wind blew with an unusual fierceness as if some greater power was urging us to move on. Spray skirts were fastened down and we shoved off in the canoes, rolling with the white-capped waves. The lake narrowed down on the approach to the Thlewiaza — the Big River — where the pull of the current wrapped itself around our canoes and tugged impatiently.

The Thlewiaza was every bit as unrestrained and reckless as a summer tornado. And we rode the backs of many frenzied rapids that coursed through bouldery chasms — runs that would surely have swamped an un-decked canoe. The rapids were short and violent but the water was high enough to carry us over ledge and boulder and spit us out into the eddy below, moments of mild terror braced by sporting blood and adrenalin.

Kasmere Lake epitomized the character of lakes in the Far North. On the tundra, wind is an omnipresent and omnipotent reality. Waves broke along boulder-strewn shallows, much like the tidal flats of Hudson Bay, making it difficult to keep close to shore or even make a safe landing. Protected camping sites could only be found in the deeper inlets that generally terminated in a sand beach where firewood was plentiful and there was some respite from the wind. There was little relief from the scourge of black flies, except in the tent or in the screened shelter I had brought along.

While searching for a place to camp on Tuninili Lake, amongst a world of ragged boulders and scabrous vegetation, we accidentally discovered a ceremonial site and amazing *dolmen stone*. Dolmen stones (from the Breton words *taol maen*, meaning "stone table"), are found worldwide and used by Aboriginal people for ceremonial purposes. A large, table-like slab of stone was usually elevated or propped up by one or more smaller stones — the cavity underneath serving as a chamber for offerings. I had seen dozens of these across the Canadian Shield but this tangerine-coloured dolmen must have weighed several tons, propped up in the air by three small rocks. In the Land of Little Sticks, there would have been no tree large enough to act as a lever to hoist up a rock this size, nor enough men with the strength to accomplish such a feat; nonetheless, it stood as a monument overlooking the lake. The colour and size of the dolmen stone matched nothing of its kind anywhere close to this site, almost as if it had been brought to this location from some great distance away, which is often the case in the North where the glaciers scooped and scraped up the thin soils and far-away boulders, later to deposit them hundreds of kilometres from their original station.

We had chosen an ancient spiritual site of some significance where huge stones were pre-arranged, facing each of the four cardinal directions, while two of the dolmens housed an array of primitive projectile points and scraping tools, placed their as offerings millennia ago.

There was a prevailing sense of novelty as we paddled this part of the northland, following a water trail that had been abandoned a century ago. The magic was everywhere, in everything we saw or touched, every day since we left Reindeer Lake. The land was strikingly beautiful and it was obvious that traffic along this route had ceased many years earlier, but traces of camp life along the trail remained. Old firepits, stone tent-rings, and esker-top graves marked with Christian-influenced picket fences stood as testimony to a hard life endured by a steadfast and proud people.

It was necessary to spend a lot of time exploring, taking notes, and locating traditional portages. When we reached the immense water of Nueltin Lake it was time to take a much needed rest. It was a hard choice to make, whether to take the time to regain our physical strength or push ahead. We were falling behind and still had three hundred kilometres to paddle before reaching the Caribou, and two weeks in which to travel in undocumented country. The rest day would grant us the needed energy it would take to make the journey.

Nueltin Lake was depicted in Farley Mowat's book *Never Cry Wolf* and appeared on the map as one of the largest lakes bordering the northern territories. Wind could have been a serious problem, but our wish came through when we rigged up our canoes again to sail in a thirty-knot wind that pushed us at a steady fifteen kilometres per hour across the bottom end of the lake — a lake that had just shed the last of its winter ice a few days before.

We headed upstream on the East River and it was obvious we were paddling a trail less travelled. As we ascended creek and river, the waters that tied the lakes together slowly diminished and we found ourselves more often waist-deep in the water hauling the canoes than paddling on top of it. The compelling scenery of tundra heath was reminiscent of pastoral Scotland (without the grazing sheep), while endless beaches rivalled any found in the Caribbean (without the palm trees). We would camp at these beaches and swim in the ice water; walk the heath behind our camp, following the tracks of moose, wolf, and caribou; catch lake trout for dinner; and marvel at the sunsets that would turn the world into a fluorescent orange diorama on its departure.

A route was located southeast from Askey Lake through several large ponds and small lakes that would link us to the White Rock River and downstream travel. This was an obscure route marked long ago by the Dene who walked here, leaving behind stone circles and quartz tooling sites; the more recent axe blazes on the few spruce and the discarded tin cans and old traps were the relics left behind by 1940s trapper Ragner Jonsson. Some of the old leg-hold traps were still staked along the tops of eskers. It was as if he had left his trap-line and camps just a few days before our arrival and would be by to collect his catch anytime soon. But that was seventy-five years ago, and the dry cold preserves the things left behind by human industry.

Blunt-leaved pondweed, herb willow, and various sedges grew tight to the lake and creek edge, sometimes making portaging difficult. The spongy bog and wet moss underfoot, and the constant wading ensured that our feet would remain soaked all day. It rained steadily for days, putting Gore-Tex jackets through the ultimate litmus test.

White Rock River eventually funneled out to Nejanalini Lake but not without first putting us through a gauntlet of steep, rock-choked rapids. The grayling were so thick in the river we would constantly hit them accidentally with our paddles, or feel them brush along our legs when we waded through the shallows. The river virtually ran out of water near the lake and we were forced to wade with the canoes out to deep water.

Nejanalini Lake appeared as an immense body of water where we could comfortably relax and enjoy not having to constantly get out of the canoes. After having been confined to small rivers and ponds over the past week, the openness of the lake was inviting, luring us out to the middle where shorelines became a faint intonation of existence. Taking advantage of the unusual calm we paddled north to the mouth of the Wolverine under the chromatic imagery of a tundra sunset, pitching camp on the flat heath between eskers sometime around midnight.

We began sighting caribou all along the Wolverine: they stopped to watch us paddle by or, from a secure distance, would watch in curiosity as we hauled our loads across the tundra between lakes. Excited beyond belief at the prospect of reaching the Roberts River — the last leg of the trip before a much needed rest day — we crossed the last tundra pond with high expectations. But the river was nowhere to be found. The shoreline was consistent except for a narrow channel that exited through a thicket of willow — not even wide enough for a canoe to fit through — and which we suspected of being the Robert's River. *It's not even a creek!* I thought.

The Robert's "River" presented different problems. There was too little water to float the canoes, and shore willows were too thick to allow us to line or even portage. For two days we either dragged our canoes over slime-encased rocks while wading in the river, watching sadly as bits of hull peeled off the canoes, or we portaged endlessly along gravelly eskers bordering the river where the wind hammered us relentlessly. The trail became obscure, water running under the rocks most of the time. Spirits waned.

We had only one day left before re-provisioning and meeting up with the rest of our group on Commonwealth Lake. As it was, we had used up our planned rest days sorely needed before starting the trek down the Caribou River. Progress was interminably slow and the Roberts River, which by now had become nothing more than a rock-infested creek, became totally un-navigable. The wind made it impossible for us to portage our canoes so we set up camp near the apex of a low esker. I thought we had done well, struggling all day with our loads over and along a non-existent river, thinking we were close to the Caribou. It was the first time I used my GPS to locate our position on the map and was astonished to see that we had only travelled four kilometres that entire day. There was still twenty kilometres to go!

Exhausted and disheartened, Jori and Walter retreated to their tent; Stephanie, who at the best of times found it difficult to cope with isolation, was beyond herself, becoming morose and argumentative. Nobody could sleep; the wind pummelled the tents without pity, threatening to shake them into oblivion, making everything seem worse.

At these times it seems hopeless that anything could change your state of affairs. There is a limit to what the body can endure, and a time when the mind can no longer rationalize such demanding needs in order to grind ahead when you're already past your limit. We lay in the tent saying nothing to each other. Not that communication was one of our strong points, anyway; silence was better than the constant barrage of negative assertions and innuendos thrown my way when things got tough. When I looked for support, there was none. That was a guide's lot, though, whether your partner was along or not. Wilderness travel is the ultimate equalizer where people are people, dealing with the same stresses and needs. There are no lawyers, or accountants, or teachers, or doctors, no wives or friends, just people living on the same plane of existence with no particular delineation. When morale slips below the horizon, for whatever reason, be it the fault of the leader or not, the collective reaction of the people is often one of blame. And if circumstances don't change, people begin challenging the authority of the guide, second-guessing his decisions on everything. Anarchy prevails.

I always remember what I learned about orienteering when I was a kid, from old Charlie the Indian, and that was to always see a trail where there was none; to be aware of the world around and the visual and audible nuances and indicators. There is always a way out of any situation before you allow fate to catch up. Antarctic explorer Ernest Shackleton knew this and was able to maintain the morale of his shipwrecked crew and bring them all to safety amidst criticism and dissention. In my mind, our situation wasn't yet critical, determined more by exhaustion than by failure or hopelessness.

Suddenly there was a clicking sound coming from across the creek that grew louder and more pronounced. "Caribou!" said a voice from the other tent. We scrambled outside. It was still light enough to clearly see the two hundred or so caribou filing along the esker on the other side of the Roberts, about a hundred metres away. They crossed the creek only metres from where our tents were pitched, an obvious caribou crossing we had inadvertently chosen to make camp on. It was a remarkable sight, an omen of good tidings which lifted our spirits, enough at least to induce conversation and hope for a better day tomorrow.

In the morning I scanned the maps and picked out a route that would get us quickly to the Caribou River where we would find deeper water. Leaving our gear in the canoes, and tying double lead-lines to the front, we were able to pull our loads across the tundra moss and grass, paddle the small heath ponds, and make it as far as the Caribou River by late afternoon. When we reached the Caribou River our hearts sank. There was no water in the upper reaches, just a trough of boulders with barely a rivulet of water between them to define its flow. It was necessary to portage the remaining five kilometres to Commonwealth Lake, over the tundra, with a strong west wind blowing.

With the canoe over my shoulders it felt like I was carrying a sheet of plywood over my head, struggling at every gust not to get blown off my feet, wrenching my back at each step, double tripping to move gear to the shore of the lake that appeared as our salvation from hard toil. The hunt-camp shack stood out on the flat horizon like a weird monument. When we did reach the lake, the paddle in deep water was a luxurious respite for blistered hands and rock-bruised feet. Sliding the canoes up on the beach at the camp, we carried our packs to the shack, headed straight for the bunks and fell asleep.

I had forgotten to pull up the canoes for the night and flip them over. In the tundra, wind can be your nemesis, while you work during the day, or while you sleep at night. If you lift your guard, forget your duties, the wilderness will make no discriminations.

One of the canoes had blown off the beach and was somewhere out on the lake. It could be anywhere. The camp was well-stocked with food, boats, and motors. Mounting one of the outboards on a small aluminum boat, Walter and I went out searching for the lost canoe. Thankfully, it had caught the edge of a small island before getting blown several kilometres down the lake. We towed it back, laughing at our luck, returning to camp just as the plane was about to land, bringing the rest of our party.

The rest of our group included the late Bob Hunter, eco-friend and co-founder of Greenpeace; a cameraman, Peter Silverman from CITY TV in Toronto; and a mystery client who had signed on late for the trip. I made arrangements with the pilot to jockey us down to Round Sand Lake, forty kilometres south along the Caribou, where I anticipated a better current flow, thus avoiding having to walk around the fifty sets of rocky rapids below Commonwealth.

The Caribou constitutes a rather small drainage basin, marked by over 250 steeply pitched rapids, tumbling 230 metres in vertical drop to Hudson Bay. Underlying bedrock has erupted onto the barren, almost treeless taiga landscape, forming magnificent mini-canyons and beautifully time-sculptured shelf-rock settings that served well as campsites.

Round Sand Lake was a shallow meteor crater four kilometres across and ringed by extensive beach formations; finding deep water anywhere on the lake was futile and we waded with our canoes for some distance before reaching a deep channel at the exit of the river. Seals had come almost 150 kilometres up the Caribou River so we were resigned to the fact that fishing from here on would not be good. Caribou were plentiful and the herds increased in size and frequency, mostly uninterested in our passing, sometimes standing along the shore watching us passively and unafraid. Sometimes only the antlers could be seen above the shore willows as small herds trailed single-file beside the river, just out of sight.

It took days to get everyone accustomed to navigating the rock-garden rapids with any kind of finesse. Although most of the rapids offered good, deep runs at the top, the terminus was often marked with a steep one to three-metre pitch-off or a pile-up of boulders where the river actually ran underneath the rocks. It was hard work for everyone, and I found myself in and out of the canoe extricating others who had broached rocks in mid-channel and couldn't get their canoes unstuck.

Peter was teamed with the mystery client who turned out to be an employee of the CIA. It was a strange match; Peter, an ex-officer of the Israeli SAS during the Seven-Days War with Egypt (currently consumer hero for CITY TV's *Silverman Helps*), and a facial reconstruction expert for the CIA and the FBI Witness Protection Program. Sam (not his real name) explicitly told everyone not to take his picture as his identity was secret and the release of any images with his face on it might get him killed. Sam made no bones about telling us stories of his exploits and having to train to endure pain by running with tacks in his shoes. But Sam was the weakest link in the group. The skills he said he had were fabricated; the gear he brought along was inadequate. Peter and Sam argued almost all the time; about who would paddle bow or stern, who would get out to line or push off rocks, to political debates about current affairs. The Caribou River resounded with the expletives of two disparately different personalities and I found myself constantly in between, mediating arguments and hauling their asses off the rocks because they were paying more attention to winning debates than getting safely through the rapids. It was, nonetheless, comic relief during hard days and everybody remained generally good-natured and compliant.

S.A. Keighley manned the Hudson's Bay Company post at Caribou Lake in the 1930s. I had brought along a copy of his book, *Trader, Tripper, Trapper: The Life of a Bay Man,* as I had planned to visit the remains of the post and it was always interesting to read about what life was like here, in such remoteness, nearly a century ago, and to see what relics might be left behind.

By sheer accident, while hiking along an esker behind our campsite, we located the HBC graveyard. It was an unusual place for a cemetery because the post itself was located some distance away. But the esker summit offered the only frost-free ground in which to dig graves deep enough to inter the dead. Time-worn picket fences, hand-hewn and scribed tomb epitaphs, stone cairns, and even the head of a Hudson's Bay issue axe lay on the ground in full view. These stark discoveries induce a residual sadness that clearly identifies the struggle for survival, not for us so much, with our techno-gear and satellite phones, but for others who lived and worked the trail; testimony of a harsh life in the wilderness and the often unforgiving "nature" of Nature.

We explored the old trade post, relegated to unpretentious, modest structures baked red-brown-grey in the sun, parched by winter dryness. Some dwellings were nothing more than a pile of dismembered sticks, but the main cabin was intact, used by the Dene as a winter stopover. A working wood stove, scattered pots, and discarded garbage defined the interior as a casual winter camp when travel across the tundra was made easy by snow machine.

The vegetation of the Taiga Shield — the alpine sweetgrass and dispensia, and Manitoba's only population of hair grass — gave way to more Arctic plain species such as sea-purslane, blue heather, and nodding saxifrage. The only thing that remained consistent were the rocks; rocks in the river rapids, rocks scattered over the tundra, rocks piled, heaved, pushed-up, and spread over the Arctic world.

At Long Lake we camped at a busy caribou crossing and watched for two days while small groups of animals swam the narrows of the lake and marched past our tents, seemingly disinterested but mildly curious as to our presence. We were nearing polar bear country and Bob began his nightly ritual of practicing defence tactics with his can of bear-spray, hunting knife, and whistle, eventually lulling himself into unconsciousness with a full ration of Wiser's Deluxe and a complement of sleeping pills and ibuprofen. We were all so river-weary that bottles of muscle relaxants and pain-killers made regular rounds, and evening imbibing of spirits and one-hour cigars became familiar companions after-hours.

The rapids became more difficult near the coast, with fewer defined deep channels and more precipitous drops. Peter and Sam were having a rough time of it until they finally overturned in a gnarly class 3 boulder garden. After extricating the canoe and paddlers from the cold water, we elected to camp high up on the riverbank along the heath plateau.

For the last day we had been paddling below the tundra, through a deep-cut trough with steep-sided gravel banks. We hauled the gear and the canoes to the top of the river bank. This gave us a panoramic view of the river and an accidental look at a strange barn-size boulder that lay on the tundra about a kilometre away on the other side of the river.

Such things demand further investigation. For the past couple of years I had been searching the Manitoba tundra for a Dene rock monument that once served as a major waymarker at a time when overland travel was the only way the people travelled. Two years earlier, Alan Code from Tadoule, on the Seal River, had asked me to keep a look out for an ancient stone or "spirit-rock" that the Dene people once used as a waymarker on their long treks across the tundra.

I took the gun as a precaution and trekked the one-kilometre distance to the huge rock; polar bears were now commonly seen further inland and had a habit of using large boulders as visual shields. Rounding the monolithic stone, a giant face appeared to be naturally contoured into the rock, as if a giant head had been neatly placed on the ground. It was the size of a small house. A quarter-ton dolmen stone had been hoisted the three or four metres up onto the crown of the headstone — the reason why from a distance it looked like a building with a chimney. It was an obvious waymarker, or possibly a spirit rock, to the travelling Dene people who once passed this way. No archaeological studies had been carried out along the river to date and this constituted a significant discovery and possibly one of Manitoba's most unique petraform sites. After the trip on the Caribou, I had collected a plethora of authenticated archaeological data, much to the chagrin of the Manitoba Archaeological Society who demanded that I hand over my findings to the government. After refusing to comply, they threatened legal action. I told them that my findings were not their intellectual or cultural property and that it belonged to the First Nations people of the province who were to receive all my data and GPS coordinates. If the government wanted the site information they would have to get it from the Dene or Cree or Saulteaux Ojibwa. It turned out that the chief archaeologists were bent out of shape because an amateur had made significant field discoveries.

The last twenty kilometres of river became an endless rock garden with braided channels not deep enough to float a canoe. Portaging was difficult over the boulders and through willow thickets in a quest to find deep water. Earlier on our last day, we had a visit by a polar bear that approached from across the river but turned away near our lunching site and wandered off downriver. That added a certain drama and tension amongst the group and Bob wouldn't go anywhere without the gun carrier close by. I carried the gun with me whenever we portaged; I didn't trust anyone else with it, particularly the CIA agent who had repeatedly asked if he could carry the shotgun. The tacks he used to put in his shoes to make him tough did nothing to prepare him adequately for the rigours of this wilderness trip.

Our rendezvous site with the outfitter was on a lake that was located one and a half kilometres off the river, to the east near Hudson Bay. We made a group pilgrimage across boggy tundra to get to a lake that didn't look as if it could receive a Beaver aircraft. Rocks and shallows seemed to plug any expanse of water; as for the outfitters cabin, it looked as if it had been abandoned years ago. The door was pulled off its mooring and the interior floor surface was two-feet-deep in insulation that had been pulled out of the walls. There were no provisions as was promised by the outfitter. This was problematic as we were guaranteed a well-equipped and supplied rendezvous camp where we could help ourselves to any food. The outfitter owned the camp on Commonwealth and it had been well-stocked, neat, and secure. There was no reason to think this camp would be any different.

We were hungry. Supplies were stretched thin, expecting a cornucopia at the end of the trail. We began to pool all our remaining food resources when the plane arrived. Four were taken out immediately to Churchill as the wind was expected to worsen by the end of the day. The pilot would return promptly to pick up the rest of us. Without admitting it, the outfitter must have felt guilty about the sad shape of his camp, knowing that he had lied about its condition. When daylight waned into evening twilight we knew the ride out wasn't forthcoming.

The time spent isolated at the cabin was necessary for me, for us all, to debrief and collect our thoughts. It was a soulful journey across the top of Manitoba. I had never been so exhausted, yet at the same time elated that we pulled it off almost precisely as planned. I slept for almost two days without eating, the others dividing out the few rations we had. I was just happy to be there, to be able to rest, like the others; and nobody had complained at all about the aloneness or the hard work of the trip. I think this was because everyone knew that when the plane finally arrived, the journey would be over. For the others, assimilation back to "civil" living would be welcome and easy. For me it just gets harder to climb back in the box with any level of concentration. I take with me the smell of saxifrage and sweetgrass, the sound of the rapids, and a visual memory of the river of stone.

Shaman's Breath by Ingrid Zschogner.

Jusquado — pine cone — keeper of the spirit rock.

©Ingrid Zschogner

SIXTEEN
PLACE OF THE HUGE ROCK LAKE

The belief in a supernatural source of evil is not necessary; men are quite capable of every wickedness.
— Joseph Conrad (1857–1924)

T wo men sat in their canoe, holding onto a shore rock, and stared up at the cliff.

"I'm going up to the top," the big man said.

"I don't think it's a good idea," his partner warned, looking concerned. The big man climbed awkwardly out of the canoe, stepped out on to a flat rock, and pulled his ball-cap tight to his forehead.

"It can't be that hard to climb … I'll get some pictures looking down. You can stay with the canoe if you want," the man chimed in as he began clambering up the broken scrabble of rock. He had no idea what he was in for; and they were both about to have the most terrifying day in their lives.

The big man was not adept at rock climbing. The base of the two-hundred-foot cliff, until about halfway up, was nothing more than chunks of granite, piled as if dumped from a huge bucket, which had settled in no orderly fashion — sharp-angled, precarious, and unstable. Luckily it had not rained, so at least the rocks were dry and the footing was good. That is, until the big man reached the cliff face, and pondered what to do next. Just above a broad platform of table rock that stood out as a promontory over the lake, the cliff was less steep and not as high; still, it was not a climber-friendly rock face. But the big man thought that if he had gotten this far, he may as well take the risk and go all the way. Somehow he managed to climb about half the way up the cliff before he suddenly stopped. The wind had picked up noticeably, the air was chilled, and a raven croaked from across the lake. The man now felt as if he had made a mistake. But it was too late.

The man sitting uneasily in the canoe watched as his friend made his way up the talus slope toward the cliff. When his friend started scaling the cliff wall, he felt more comfortable with the canoe tied up, and continued to watch from the shore. A fresh breeze came up and pulled at the canoe, causing it to bang against the rocks. It was all too unsettling. There was a strangeness to the air and it felt wrong to be in this place. He called to his friend to come back. What he saw next made him stomach lurch. The cliff face, against which his friend was clinging, suddenly pulled out from the rest of the wall. It hung momentarily, suspended it seemed by invisible hands, and then began to crumble and separate. The massive rock buttress broke away from the cliff, carrying the big man with it, tossing him like a rag doll, over and under disintegrating granite until he disappeared several metres into the settled scree. The man with the canoe gasped, not really knowing what to do, waiting for a call from his friend to say that he was alright, maybe a few scratches, that's all. He yelled to his friend but received no answer. Dust from the rock fall was still settling, the wind had subsided, and there was an eerie stillness that made the canoe man tremble. He climbed the slope toward the rock fall and his friend. There were huge gaps between the boulders. Cold, damp air emanated from dark voids and rocks teetered nervously on questionable perches; at best, firm footing was elusive. He was now close enough to hear moaning. At least his friend was alive. The man had not been pinned under boulders, luckily, but he had suffered a badly crushed leg and one hand looked as if it had gone through a meat grinder … bad luck for a concert pianist.

The large man outweighed his partner by nearly fifty pounds. The trip back down off the scree would be difficult, as it was hard enough getting up to where they were. For hours the two men worked their way back down to the canoe and then to the portage at the end of the small lake. It was nearly a kilometre to Obabika Lake, then a fifteen-kilometre paddle to yet another kilometre portage that would take them into Lake Temagami and help. They weren't equipped with a satellite phone; all they could do was to paddle hard to get out. By nightfall they had reached Lake Temagami. They waved frantically at passersby in fishing boats but all they did was wave back and motor on without stopping. Finally, reaching an occupied cottage, they managed to talk the owner into boating them back to their car at the landing.

These men rented a canoe from me back when I was in the outfitting business. I knew nothing of their intentions and, had I known that an attempt would be made to climb Chee-skon-abikong Cliff, I would have advised them not to do it. Not just because they lacked climbing experience, but because of the spiritual nature of this place, in that the lake was sacred to the Anishnabe and still held potent spirit energy. It was one of the most beautiful places I knew, but it also had an enigmatic nature about it that was somehow dangerous, but dangerous only to the uninitiated or irreverent. I paddled in to the site a few days later to observe what had happened. Somehow I felt that it was partly my fault, him being there, almost dying. I found his ball-cap sitting amongst the freshly broken rock. Unlike the cliff itself, festooned with rock tripe and lichen, grey like barn-board from the sun, the new rock was golden yellow with traces of azure-blue and obvious grains of silica and quartz, clean and rain-washed, piled untidily over the old rock. The rock fall had been massive ... the man should have died but he hadn't. *How did he survive?*

The conjuring rock was behind me, about fifty metres away. Below was the ceremonial rock terrace that stood just above the treetops. Here the pines were twelve stories high but you still looked down on them from the stone platform. The rock fall had spilled stone cubes and chunks as far down as the platform terrace. I climbed through the rubble, up onto the ceremonial terrace, sat down, and looked out over the lake. There was an obvious and unsettling character to the breeze that was now coursing along the escarpment. There was beauty here, and like a lot of places in the Canadian Shield landscape, this glorification also ennobles a strong spiritual acclaim.

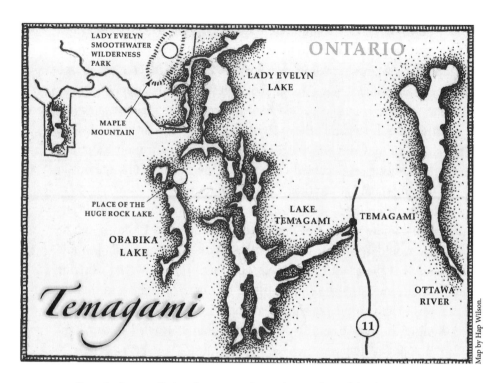

Map by Hap Wilson.

I took the medicine bag out of my daypack and laid it out in front of me, beside an old ring of stones that encircled an ancient fireplace long since abandoned. I came here as often as I could, just to sit quietly, reflect, and to let life's anxieties ooze out of my soul. I lit the cedar and sweetgrass smudge-stick and set it down in the fireplace, closed my eyes, and tried to think of what happened here a few days ago, and why this man was allowed to live when in all right he should have been crushed to death under tons of rock. And then the answer came to me. It was a healing place; a place where life was refreshed and renewed, not a place of death or destruction. The event was a caveat, perhaps a forewarning of events to come, the clouds on the horizon. Beauty comes with a price tag, and the forests here were sought-after by logging companies.

One hundred and eighteen years ago, a Teme-Augama Anishnabe Elder named Windaban gave Robert Bell, a famous surveyor at the time, a hand-sketched depiction of the Temagami region showing local place names.

One place of prominent importance was Chee-skon-abikong sakahegan, or, for those not fluent in Ojibwa, "conjuring rock place lake." Chee-skon Lake is about 135 kilometres north of North Bay, within the famed Temagami wilderness area, adjacent to one of the more popular canoe routes in northeast Ontario. From Obabika Lake, an 850-metre portage, mostly uphill, ends abruptly at a Windex-blue lake, rimmed along the east shore by an impressive seventy-metre-high escarpment. The lake is small, less than a kilometre long, but everything else is gargantuan, particularly the 350-year-old ancient forest of white and red pine. The portage is part of the five-thousand-year-old Nastawgan, or aboriginal trail system, still in use by infrequent canoeists but mostly by resident moose and bear. Pileated woodpeckers, thrushes, barred owls, and pine marten are as numerous here as city pigeons. Near the end of the lake, perched precariously along the top line of scree, is the conjuring rock — a free-standing pillar of stone that visually disappears against the cliff backdrop on sunless days.

Anishnabe linguistic expert and historian Craig Macdonald says of Chee-skon, "The name is derived from the root word for 'shaking tent' — the seven-poled, open-topped shelter used by medicine healers (shamans)." Chee-skon was, and still is, a place of powerful divination. Small, bowl-sized depressions surrounding the base of the thirty-metre-high column of rock are naturally filled with water; people seeking visions or healing sat at these pools and stared into the future in a trance-like state. Nearby, the rock outcrop or terrace was used for vision seeking and acts of reverence — a place for offerings. The campsite across the strikingly clear blue lake faces the escarpment and the omnipresent conjuring rock, most visible when shadows are cast by the late afternoon sun.

I first saw the conjuring rock while on a three-month winter camping expedition when I was twenty-one, in 1974. My friend and I had been breaking a trail, exhausted from hauling heavily laden toboggans, coming down from our base camp at Diamond Lake which was some distance to the north. We were heading to Bear Island Reserve for supplies that we would purchase from the Hudson's Bay store. The route chosen was obscure and not the shortest distance to the post according to our maps. But at that age we were looking more for adventure than any shortcut. There were old portages along this route but they were heavily overgrown and tangled with deadfall and deep with mid-winter snow. Upon reaching Chee-skon we could go no further without resting. Lighting a fire for snow-tea, we sat on our toboggan loads under the snow-crusted branches of giant pines, regaining our strength to go on. The conjuring rock did not show itself that day, as it was cloudy and shadowless, nevertheless I remember feeling a sense of peace as I sat there sipping hot tea and remarking to my friend how stunning the scene was. It meant little to me then, not knowing its full import as a spiritual place and sacred forest, but I would remember Chee-skon as a place where I found strength when I had little energy left to push on. A decade later I would be back, for another purpose, to seek an angle or leverage that might work to change the course of politics that governed forestry practices in Temagami and in the province of Ontario.

In 1986, the politics of wilderness compromised the secretness of this place. Natives and environmentalists reluctantly brought this pristine gem into the public eye in order to save it. Although the west coast gained world recognition for its disappearing old-growth cedars — in the Carmanah and Stein Valley area of British Columbia — old-growth forests in Ontario were not recognized. Pine forests whose age exceeded one hundred years were considered "decadent" and ripe for clear-cutting. Old trees or old forests were considered valueless unless "harvested" and shipped to mills. Pine forests in central Canada had all but disappeared, except in choice places like Temagami. Timber mills were hungry to cut down the last of them ... and the Ontario government foresters were quick to stamp their approval on cutting permits to allow for such ecological genocide.

Brian Back, the executive director for our newfound group, the Temagami Wilderness Society, met me at the north end of Obabika Lake, at a campsite near the foot of the portage to Chee-skon Lake. We had discussed the idea of creating a symbolic issue that would vault our group into the forefront of the environmental movement with the purpose of saving the wilderness canoe routes of Temagami. We didn't have the backing of the collective canoeing fraternity (except for Camp Keewaydin) — the historic canoe camps were mostly American owned and they didn't want to get directly involved, and the provincial and federal canoeing organizations derived a good percentage of their funding from government sources. One of the hallmark features of Temagami, of which there were several to choose from, was the huge white pine stands that defined the character of the landscape and the canoeing experience. We determined then and there that the Province would be forced to adopt a policy on old-growth forest for the province of Ontario, and we were going to do it using the Obabika pine forests to prove our point.

I had mentioned to Back that the small lake northeast of Obabika was one of the most beautiful places I had found in the district, and persuaded him to check it out with me. The portage trail was lined with ancient red pines and had been used for the last five thousand years by the local Anishnabe. On Chee-skon Lake we paddled along the cliff-side shore, but it wasn't until we pulled away from the foot of the escarpment that we noticed the column of rock perched in front of the cliff. The sun had defined the rock in shadowed bas relief, magnificent and unusual in stark contrast to the backdrop of granite. Paddling over to the nearby campsite, Brian and I sat in awe, excited, elated to finally see what lay ahead of us. It was at this place that ideas were born and the vision set in motion to identify Temagami as the "Last Stand" to protect the ancient old-growth forests. And Chee-skon Lake and the conjuring rock would be the polarizing image to work into the minds of those who took that stand.

Later, Craig Macdonald would verify for us that Chee-skon abikong was one of the most revered spiritual sites in the province. Independent foresters, or those not on government payrolls, would acclaim the Obabika forests as one of the largest contiguous stands of old-growth red and white pine trees in the world.

But there was a price to pay for such notoriety. Before the threat of logging earmarked Chee-skon for prominence as an environmental tool, it was known only to a paltry few canoeists, mostly from Camp Keewaydin on Lake Temagami, who sent boys through the old canoe portage route once every couple of years. It was one of those out-of-the-way cross-over routes that deflected most canoe traffic because the portages were long; uphill when coming from the south, boggy on the middle portage, and another nearly two-kilometre carry in or out of Diamond Lake. Too much work for the modern paddler. But in the mid-1980s, the environmental movement was in full swing and saving

Canadian old-growth forests was a sexy issue for the greens ... and we stroked it as far as we could. Trails were built (some illegally), stands were tree-spiked, approaching logging road bridges were burned out, Natives and whites blockaded roads, the aspiring soon-to-be Ontario premier would get hauled off by police, Robert Bateman and most of Canada's best nature artists camped out there, and media buzzed around Temagami like a disturbed hornets' nest.

Within two weeks of signalling the public about Chee-skon Lake and the old-growth forests, photographers and curious paddlers set their compasses for Obabika Lake. Carelessly discarded film wrappers, food packaging, and other human detritus started appearing at the base of old trees and along portage and hiking trails. Nearby campsites began to fill up and human waste was not properly disposed of. The TWS (Temagami Wilderness Society) did its best to impress upon visitors the need to uphold the acceptable wilderness code of ethics, but humans do have a way of "loving things to death." And I was a part of the problem. I gladly rented canoes to those who wanted to visit the site, and the more people we pushed through, the stronger our support grew, the more memberships we sold, and the greater our effort to protect the wilderness. But it was a double-edged sword we were wielding; in the process of protecting what we loved, we actually compromised its secretness and vulnerability as a sacred place. But what were our choices? Notoriety and protected forests, a scant bit of garbage left behind by inconsiderate campers, or clear-cut wasteland? Not quite a moral dilemma, at least for those with preservationist leanings, but there were moments when I cast doubts on our methodology. When the shrill, incongruous voices bellowed across the Chee-skon landscape and the impious tracked upon the sacred boulders, noisily clambering about the scree looking for artifacts and answers, I'm sure it made the gods shudder.

I spent ten days at Chee-skon with a Celtic Druid shaman named Marish, in 1994. He had never been to Canada. He had been around the world to many revered sacred places but Chee-skon, he said, was truly one of the more powerful divining wonders: "The resonance of spiritual power here is strong ... but if the land is disturbed [by logging or development] the resident spiritual entity removes itself and searches elsewhere for peace."

I wondered if we had already gone too far, and if by developing the place as an eco-adventure destination, we had despoiled its inherent richness as a sacred place and that its healing power had been sacrificed for public notice. These thoughts linger, although I have seen the devastation wrought by clear-cut logging across the back of Mother Earth and I am reminded of the importance of Chee-skon, spiritually, and for its spectacular ecosystem. There are very few places like this one left on the planet.

Alex Mathias, an almost legendary Anishnabe protector of Wendaban Territory — his traditional hunting grounds — lives near Chee-skon at the mouth of the Obabika River. He decided to live off the Bear Island Reserve on Lake Temagami, to keep the family traditional land occupied and, for the most part, lives off the land by trapping, hunting, and fishing. His Native name, Coming of the Clouds, has an almost prophetic, hopefully not apocalyptic, reference to the approaching storm of protest that still lingers around Chee-skon. Logging companies continue to press the government for access to the rich timber above the sacred escarpment; boardroom fights persist between bureaucrats and environmentalists — the browns rationalizing cutting Chee-skon to pacify commercial demands, and the greens maintaining an emotional, psychological plea to save a cultural and ecological wonder.

Alex worries that the movement of heavy machinery behind the great cliff will cause the conjuring rock to slip off its moorings. At one time, in the not too distant past, there were three conjuring stones at Chee-skon-abikong; two have since collapsed into the rubble at the base of the cliff, and only the one remains. Visitors who walk the trails here leave prayer flags amongst the giant pines and along the cliff overlooks, hoping for some miracle that will save this place. Its fate rests, not in the hands and hearts of the people of Ontario, the democratic process long ago abandoned in such matters, but in the stroke of a pen that will sanction, yet again, a done-deal between government foresters and industry, based solely on principle. The fear that losing a proposed cutting area will set a dangerous precedent is strong. The destiny of Chee-skon, like any remaining pocket of spiritual wilderness, will be decided upon and protected only if the bureaucrats and industry leaders sensitize themselves to such issues. And that's likely not to happen anytime soon.

The trail is not a self-seeking goal but the journey that unfolds getting there.

SEVENTEEN
CHEE-BAY-JING

May your trails be crooked, winding, lonesome, dangerous, leading to the most amazing view. May your mountains rise into and above the clouds.

— Edward Abbey

*H*ave you outlived your soul? Have you *outlived* your soul?

"Bob, read this." I pointed to the ceiling of the fire tower cupola where someone had carved the epigram. Bob Hunter was just climbing through the man-hole from the tower ladder and looked up.

"Christ, isn't that prophetic," Bob exclaimed. It wasn't your usual hastily carved witticism one would normally find on a cabin wall. There were hundreds of signatures, aphorisms, graffiti, and a few token obscenities … and one mystical revelation scratched in or scribbled in pen or marker on every square inch of wall and ceiling space in the tiny tower lookout cabin.

We were over a hundred feet up, suspended by four steel legs whose base plates were slowly detaching from their crumbling foundation. The ladder was enclosed in a hooped tunnel but several of the rings had come loose from their moorings. As you climbed higher the wind increased incrementally, shaking the whole structure and making you wish you had kept your feet on the ground. The cabin itself was a plywood box, about eight-foot square, ringed with windows, and topped off with a gambrel roof. The tower hadn't been officially occupied for half a century.

Most fire towers in Ontario were erected between 1920 and 1950. The towerman was seasonally employed from May to October. Originally, lookout rangers were positioned alone, for months at a time. But the government found that many men were incapable of coping with the isolation; some rangers went crazy, committed suicide, or walked off the job, and the men who would often sign up for the job were already a bit neurotic. The government then started to allow towermen to bring their families along and improved living conditions substantially. Fires were located by using two towers, giving the location of a fire on the map based on a 360 degree radius. The tool they used to spot a "smoke" was called an alidade and was mounted on a circular table with a map of the area and an azimuth-ring to plot the fire direction. The tower was the centre point of the map. The observer reported the compass direction, distance, and size of the fire to headquarters by "bush phone lines" in the earlier years, and then by two-way radio in later years.

Towers were erected in about two weeks. The steel pieces weren't that heavy so each section could be bolted together easily. The construction process wasn't for the feint of heart, though once the tower rose above the treetops, it got a little bit trickier. The top cabins or cupolas were hoisted up piece-by-piece and bolted at the joints. Earlier towers that used lighter gauge steel had a tendency to sway in the wind. Some even toppled over during storms.

During my stint as a park ranger, and while mapping out Temagami for a trails guidebook, I had visited one of the district's last occupied towers at Pinetorch Lake. A fire had ripped through the forest near the lake, obliterating the original trail to the tower. The tower had been spared. Charting out a new trail to the summit of the tower hill, from a different direction and about three kilometres distant, my crew and I brushed out a rough path on the unburned side of the ridge. It was a difficult process but we made it to the tower in about six hours. Climbing to the top and entering the cupola I saw that the sighting table was intact, just as it had been at the time the tower was in service twenty years earlier. Knowing that many of Ontario's towers were being dismantled for liability reasons, I decided to liberate the table and carry it out. It was dismantled and lowered to the ground with a rope. The steel pedestal table support was not light, neither was the wooden table, intact with alidade and azimuth-ring and original sighting map. It was a treasure and probably one of the last remaining sighting tables left in the country. We carried it the three kilometres back to our campsite and then portaged and paddled it another ten kilometres to where the government plane picked us up later that week.

I remember seeing my first fire tower when I was six years old — a tall wooden structure that was being built by my uncle who was employed by the Department of Lands & Forests. That was in the 1950s. Ten years later, I was canoeing in Algonquin Park and came across a recently abandoned fire tower. It was a shaky structure with guy-lines that fluttered and swayed aimlessly, too slack to be of any service. The ladder had no safety hoop behind it. Four of us climbed the tower and I remember being terrified but too stubborn to back down. Inside the cupola, the last ranger had left a notebook full of poetry behind, most of it too profound for us to have understood then, except that it had the word "death" outlined on every page.

Bob and I sat on the floor of the tower pondering the quote on the ceiling. *Have you outlived your soul?*

"Shit, Bob, do you think there's a point in our life when the soul just gives up?" I queried, knowing that Bob was a keen believer in two things; that he was reincarnated from something far less abstract, and that he was from another planet and that his "ship" was about to arrive any day to pick him up. Bob Hunter, the environmental icon who gave birth to the Greenpeace organization in 1972, had already lived several lives, all at once, and he surmised that he may have expended his "soul" purpose on this particular planet. Bob had been ill and would soon find out that he had prostate cancer.

I was running an expedition in Temagami, Ontario, for CITY TV and Bob Hunter was doing an in-your-face exposé of clear-cut logging of the old-growth pine forests. Maple Mountain was one of Temagami's hallmark features; from the summit you could see the areas slated for invasive logging which was about to take place. Bob was shooting a mini-documentary to be aired at the Toronto station and the mountain was a key spot to do a standup interview. Bob had some difficulty on the four-kilometre trail on the way up, and the one-hundred-foot-climb up the tower ladder just about did him in.

Sitting for a while in the cupola of the tower, contemplating the general state of affairs, Bob caught his breath enough to recite his lines for the interview. I was busy slinging the heavy camera up the ladder by rope, trying not to bang it on the edges of the safety barrier. The cameraman followed his camera up the ladder and joined us in the cupola.

It was a calm afternoon, comparatively, but I always felt nervous once you crammed more than two people up in the tiny space of the cupola; every movement caused a ricochet of vibration. Even though it was a newer tower, there were no supporting cables tethered off the four sides like some of the old ones, and all I could think of was the crumbling foot plates around the tower's steel legs.

"How safe is this tower?" asked the cameraman. He was nervous, making any move with a reserved caution that made us all a bit edgy.

"It's as solid as the day it was erected, don't worry," I lied. Bob tried to open one of the Plexiglas windows and the jarring caused the window frame to come loose.

"Don't touch anything!" I told them, a little too over-excited, and everybody froze. This just accentuated every rattle and shake in the tower structure, adding to the tension. The interview was brief, punchy, and carried out with a dearth of movement. The trip down the ladder was always more difficult; once outside the cupola you were blasted by wind and forced to view the world from a less secure place ... like holding on to the outside of a balcony railing, ten stories up.

Bob Hunter got his story and broadcast it to the couple-hundred thousand people dedicated to the new media zone, replete with jerky camera shots and on-the-fly interviews and video clips of desiccated and ravaged forests.

Political issues affecting the cultural and ecological attributes of Temagami were not a new or trendy item, sparked by a handful of radical hippy environmentalists. To the Teme-Augama Anishnabe, or "Deep Water People," Temagami was part of a ten-thousand-square-kilometre area known as *n'Daki-Menan*, meaning "Our Land." This wilderness has been the homeland of the TAA for five thousand years; their Aboriginal trail system known as the Nastawgan constitutes one of the largest, still intact networks of trails found on the planet. After Canadian Confederation in 1867, the TAA found themselves in dispute over the ownership of their ancestral lands, not having signed any treaty giving ownership away. During the Robinson-Huron Treaty era, when a bonified chief or representative of a band could not be located, government officials would appoint someone to sign in their stead, often with the help of cheap rum. In the ensuing years, there were repeated appeals by the TAA to the government of Ontario, and subsequently to the federal government, to recognize Aboriginal ownership of lands within the Temagami region. Although logging didn't take place in Temagami until the late 1920s, it nevertheless made Ontario's position on the rights of the TAA very transparent. The government wasn't about to relinquish any pine-rich lands to the local Natives. In 1943, the federal government did herd the TAA onto a small reserve on Bear Island in central Lake Temagami but made no motion to settle their land claim.

The dispute intensified in 1972, when the Ontario government, backed by self-assuming local politicians, announced plans for the construction of a world-class ski resort on Maple Mountain. The mountain was one of Ontario's loftiest peaks, rising over a thousand feet above the surrounding lakes. Although ranking thirteenth highest in elevation above sea level, its vertical height above the surrounding countryside makes it the loftiest of Ontario's top twenty-five "mountains." It would have been the province's highest vertical ski run. It was a grandiose and costly scheme, not well-conceived or thought through with any level of professional attention. Promises of local employment kept the local politicians snarling with high expectations. Unrealistic and contrived as the promises may have been, the carrot still dangled enough to keep developers at odds with both the TAA and the now-burgeoning environmental movement.

The Natives were all fired up and with good reason: Maple Mountain was known to them for millennia as *Chee-Bay-Jing,* or "the place where the soul spirit goes after the body dies," and it was tribal custom to lay bodies at the foot of the mountain. After more than a century of frustration, the Temagami Natives initiated legal action in 1973 by placing a formal "caution" on 111 townships within their prescribed homeland. This legal caution froze all new land sales and mineral staking, and silenced the Maple Mountain ski resort project. Unfortunately, it was business as usual for the logging companies, and the companies wanted Temagami pine.

By the mid 1970s, little of the original pine forest remained in the rest of Ontario; Temagami owned impressive old-growth white and red pine stands and the logging industry now set its target here, consolidated by a rubber-stamped deal endorsed by the Ministry of Natural Resources. New logging roads were approved and cutting licences issued. The battle began.

But this story isn't about the environmental movement, or the Native Land Claim, or even the ten deaths that have taken place on the mountain over the last few decades. It's really about a trail, and where that trail leads. It's what Maple Mountain, or Chee-Bay-Jing, means to any number of singular individual efforts — it's about a magnetism that draws people to make the pilgrimage to the summit, for whatever purpose.

Collectively, there are a thousand stories to be told about Maple Mountain. High places have attracted people since the beginning of humankind. Maple Mountain affords relatively easy access for a high quality wilderness experience, and people from around the globe make the trek to its apex each summer.

The first non-Aboriginal to climb the mountain was Dr. Robert Bell of the Geological Survey of Canada, in 1888. Bell, dubbed the "father of place names," was considered one of Canada's greatest exploring scientists, having named over three thousand geological features, mostly mapping the rivers between Hudson Bay and Lake Superior. Bell's trek up the mountain pre-dated the fire tower era; he likely made the climb with local Anishnabe guides or bushwhacked to the top of his own accord. Bell named the mountain for its unusually extensive stands of hardwood trees, mostly maples, which grew along the east slope of the mountain.

There used to be trees growing on the top of the mountain. In the years just prior to the disbanding of the tower program, the fire ranger

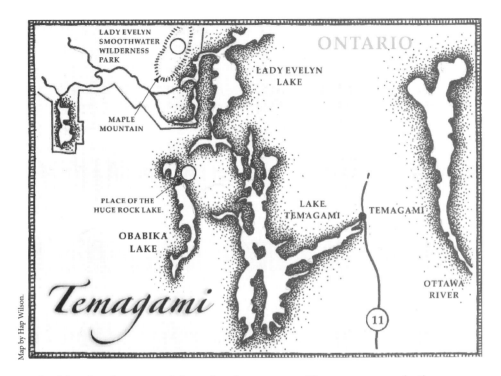

Map by Hap Wilson.

had his family stay with him for the summer. The government built an additional ranger shack on the summit, beside the tower, so the ranger didn't have to make the four-kilometre hike each day down to the base of the trail. Fuel and other supplies were occasionally dropped by helicopter. Gas spills were frequent. While playing around the fuel shed, one of the ranger's children had been playing with matches and a fire erupted that ravaged the entire summit. Trees never grew back but the blueberries were incredibly profuse afterwards.

Before becoming a ranger in Temagami in 1977, I had climbed the mountain a couple times while on extensive canoe trips. The old ranger trail from Tupper Lake was barely traceable and few people climbed the mountain just because of the difficulty in finding the trail entrance. One of my first jobs as a canoe ranger was to improve the Maple Mountain tower trail; canoeists had been complaining constantly about the condition of the trail to head office. I had also featured the mountain hike as one of the primary attractions in the recently released guidebook, hoping to get more people up the mountain in an attempt to prove to the government that paddlers don't always stick to the water trails. Bureaucrats based their protective no-cut reserves along recreation trails by the intensity of use. Their argument that logging companies should be able to cut close to shorelines because canoeists stick to the water routes only, didn't hold water in Temagami — there were over three-dozen highpoints in the district, any one of which canoeists could climb to get a panoramic view, but of what … clear-cuts?

My crew and I spent a week brushing out the trail, shouldering in lumber for boardwalks over wet bog and to build a bridge over a small creek. The wood was flown in to Forestry Island on Sucker Gut Lake, about fifteen kilometres away, and then transported by motorboat to the trailhead at the old ranger cabin on Tupper Lake. The boat trip in each day had been difficult, having to drag the boat over rocky shallows, sand bars, and beaver dams along Willow Island Creek. Black flies and mosquitoes had been particularly irksome because of the June rains, and in July it was scorching hot, making it tough work hiking up the mountain with lumber over your shoulder.

We arrived at the mountain trailhead each morning to see canoes pulled up on shore. Paddlers from various camps had been making the hike for decades, but now, since the word got out that the trail was being improved, it seemed everybody with a canoe made a bee-line to the mountain. It took most of the morning for four of us to move about a half a ton of lumber a kilometre and a half up the trail; steady trips up and down, collapsing in the cold-water spring at the bottom between each trip. The heat was unbearable.

There were fresh footprints going up the mountain but by late afternoon no one had come back down. Beyond our bridge construction, the trail makes abrupt inclines, sometimes requiring steady footing and both hands to pull yourself up ledges or over boulder piles. Near the top, it's necessary to climb a steel ladder up an almost vertical rock face, followed by an unstable goat track to the summit. It's considered one of the most difficult hikes in the province.

We were just about to pack it up for the day when we heard a distinct banging noise from up the trail. It sounded like the gunnels of an aluminum canoe hitting rocks and trees, which was absurd because this was obviously not a portage. Listening to this for some time and the noise getting nearer, now with a complement of curses and shouts, we decided to see what or who was coming down from the summit. A man carrying a sixteen-foot aluminum canoe appeared across the creek and, because the bridge was not yet finished, had to wade knee-deep in virtual muskeg to reach us at the other side. The man was followed by his canoe partner carrying a lunch pack. Both paused for a few moments but the man never put down his canoe.

"What are you doing … you guys lost?" I asked. The young man with the canoe tilted it back to look at me.

"I'm the first person to carry a canoe all the way to the top and back," he exclaimed with a certain amount of pomp. It was quite a feat; an eight-kilometre quest accomplished in thirty-degree weather. He looked just about done in.

"No, you're not," I replied with an almost morbid pleasure.

"What do you mean?"

"A canoe guide from Camp Keewaydin did it a year ago," I told him.

"What?" His face started to turn even redder.

"He also had a fifty-pound pack on his back," I added. It was true. I didn't have to tell him. I could have spared him the humility and deflated ego, but I had distaste for self-indulgent goal seekers with a conquer-it attitude and this guy had no interest in anything but his accomplishment. Angry, he threw his canoe down on the rocks and pummeled it with his feet until his partner stopped him. They both carried it the rest of the way down the mountain.

Outrageous actions create outrageous events. People enter the wilderness with preconceived ideas and aspirations, often for particular reasons that are vainglorious with no benefit to others and no respect for the land. It has been the habit of some adventurers to use sacred places specifically to flaunt their ignorance. The young man with the canoe had no outward effect other than humbling his own pride; some take the time to make the climb with the sole purpose of self adulation.

I've climbed the mountain trail dozens of times over the years, each time an enlightening experience; I see something new each time that I had missed on previous trips to Chee-Bay-Jing, sometimes things that raise the spirit and sometimes things that penetrate the heart. It has been on too many recent occasions when I reach the summit to see some sort of graffiti scribbled over the east-facing cliffs, or childish hand-scratchings over the table rock around the tower. I remind myself that it's a product of the times and the lure of famous places always attracts a maudlin crowd. There are those who seek nothing more than an opportunity to see the world from a higher place, to feast on wild blueberries, to bask in the summer sun after an arduous trek, perhaps to seek a vision as the Anishnabe did over the centuries past.

I had my own obsessions. The first time up the mountain as a ranger I was guiding the district planner, a summer student, and my wife on an exploratory trip and we had decided to carry our camping gear to the top and spend the night. My wife was afraid of heights so she pitched her tent below the tower while the rest of us carried our sleeping bags up the ladder to the cupola.

It was a clear evening with traces of diminishing afternoon clouds; enough definition to accentuate the sunset in its whole array of colours. Time passed and the sun went down. Having imbibed several cups of tea at the base camp before climbing the tower, the three of us now had to urinate but none of us wanted to make the long descent down the ladder. We decided to open the windows on one side of the cupola, away from my wife's tent, and relieve ourselves. It all seemed to be planned out with simple logic; however, the breeze that was now coming from the north blew the effluent directly onto the tent below in three long, steaming streams. My wife, surprised that it was raining on a clear night, stuck her head out the door and looked up, only to get the full force of three men urinating from ten stories up. Curses and threats of vengeance were lost amongst a volley of chortles and cat calls from above.

We had spread out our sleeping bags on the floor of the cupola; the light wind playing music in the tower superstructure soon sent a reverberation up through the floor of the cabin, shaking and rattling without pause, sounding like macabre music emanating from the bones of a giant rib cage. It was unnerving. I couldn't help but think of the Ojibwa creature Paguk, a supernatural being very much feared amongst the Anishnabe. Paguk is a monster of bones, a skeleton that clatters through the forest making a great rattling and squeaking noise. Once a hunter, Paguk got lost and starved to death, but before he died he wished that his life and the strength of his flesh might be transferred to his bones. He got his wish, and his strength went into his bones when his flesh fell away. Whenever he wished, he could fly through the air as though on wings. It is thought that if the rattling of his bones is heard three times in succession; once at the horizon, once at the zenith, and again at the opposite horizon, it is a sign that someone will die.

In the middle of the night there was a loud scream. Three of us sat bolt upright grabbing on to the walls of the cupola to brace ourselves. *The tower's coming down,* I thought. I waited for the whine of twisted metal and the quick plummet to earth. Nothing happened. It was relatively quiet save for the modest rocking of the tower.

"Nightmare, sorry guys ... bad dream," the student confessed. My heart was still pounding. I lay there, cramped and uncomfortable, for hours it seemed, until the first light of morning. Watching the sun rise over the Temagami wilderness from such a height was worth the bad sleep but I swore I would never do this again.

Ten years later I was back, this time with a girlfriend (yes, I was now divorced, but not because I pissed on my wife), who was keen on making the trek up the mountain; she also insisted we spend the night in the tower. It was a year before a lightning blast ignited a wildfire on the summit less than a kilometre from the tower. The weather was sketchy, unsettled, the wind not quite knowing which way to blow. It was one of those warm May days that usually induced a bad storm, cold air mixing with the hot air from the south that almost always erupted into a half gale. Gut feeling told me that leaving our comfortable and secure campsite on nearby Hobart Lake was a bad idea. Regardless, we packed a night kit, some snacks, and headed over to the trailhead in late afternoon.

Maple Mountain has a peculiar character to its weather, be it the cause of such vertical abruptness in the topography, or perhaps something more metaphysical in explanation. While it may be warm and windless at the base of the mountain, cloudless and perfect in all respects, by the time you clear the treeline and heavy canopy after about an hours trek, the weather may have turned to the worse. Caught unprepared, there is a chance of a good soaking, the subsequent chill, and the threat of hypothermia before you get back to your canoe and campsite. Of the fifty or so times I have been up the mountain, it has almost always been windy, clear sky or not. You just know to take the appropriate gear with you when you make the hike.

When my friend and I climbed to the bare ridge there was hardly a breeze blowing. It was unseasonably warm, hazy, and thick with black flies. Mock suns had formed on both sides of the sun — a "sun dog" — an atmospheric optical phenomena produced by the refraction of sunlight through ice crystals in cirrostratus clouds. That usually means rain within the next twelve hours. Our view of the surrounding wilderness was diminishing steadily as the day wore on. It was a bleak landscape, almost monochromatic with the grey haze and the leafless trees of early spring. There were no blueberries to pick or endless vistas to wonder at, or cheery sunshine to bask in; eventually, fog obscured the view from the summit completely until even the top of the tower became invisible.

The dampness started eating into our stiffening joints and there was no firewood close at hand without a lot of work, and I hadn't brought an axe or a saw with me. The only thing to do was to climb the tower and use the shelter to ward off the chill, get into our sleeping bags and try to sleep. Déjà vu ... I had been here before and I didn't enjoy the experience, and here I was doing it again. Climbing the tower into the heavy fog felt as if we were about to become sacrificial offerings to the gods. The weather could change quickly up here and it wouldn't be for the better. And towers get struck by lightning a lot; why wouldn't they? We were a couple of flies stuck on the top of a one-hundred-foot antenna.

I was prepared for a fitful sleep and that's exactly what I got. There was a peculiar stillness to the tower. It made no sound. If it had, I probably would have fallen asleep. Instead I just lay there, listening to my own breathing. Sometime during the night I had drifted off but awoke to a distant sound, like the low hum of an approaching motorboat, but there weren't any boats on the lakes nearby, especially at night. The noise increased and I realized it was the wind playing against the steel frame of the tower. By three in the morning the tower was about to rattle off its footings, the wind coming in violent and persistent waves with intermittent sheets of cold rain blowing in through the broken Plexiglas windows. We pushed our sleeping bags to the middle of the cupola but couldn't escape the drizzle that settled on everything. The clattering became so loud we couldn't hear ourselves speak as we huddled together to stay warm, sleeping bags now packed away and ready for our escape as soon as the morning light appeared.

When morning did come it crept ever so slowly over the horizon, only to be blotted out by approaching storm clouds. Thunder rolled through the valleys, pushing its way along the ridge and the tower. It was time to go. Holding on to the ladder handrails was difficult in the wind, the metal was cold and the pack on my back kept getting jammed in the safety bars behind me. We escaped the tower before the full force of the storm hit and we took shelter under a rock overhang below the east-facing cliff. The ridge and tree cover offered some respite from the thunderstorm but we were both quite chilled, deciding to make the hike down the mountain to keep warm. Once at the trailhead and the lake edge, it was if we had re-entered a different world altogether. The sun was shining, the wind had abated, birds were singing.

Paddling back to the campsite I looked back at Chee-Bay-Jing rising out of the surrounding forest, painted gold by the morning sun, aglow from the spring rain, the dark clouds, feathered and broken, drifting off to the south. It was a burial site, a place where the spirit dwells after death; maybe Paguk himself wanders the mountain in search of his own lost soul, or has outlived it, like the rest of us.

Merganser.

Blackwater Reflections by Hap Wilson.

AFTERWORD

The trail is the thing, not the end of the trail. Travel too fast and you miss all you are travelling for.
— Louis L'Amour (1908–1988), *Ride the Dark Trail*

Wonderful forest trails that were very much a part of my life while growing up, and had been for others before me for nearly a hundred years, are now grown over, covered with forest slough and new growth. Today, nearby, live at least a hundred or so children, none of whom play along the trails like I did, like my friends did. Children aren't interested in exploring anymore, and parents are loath to allow them such freedom. It isn't safe to allow kids to roam alone and parents are too busy to accompany them.

The world is small and wilderness is diminishing. Trails are being replaced by roads. And with this new reality comes a proliferation of adventure-seekers and survivalist addicts looking for boxed and packaged experiences. As adventure tourism grows, so too does the frequency of misadventure. It's a time of facades, perceptions, and quick fixes. People hunger for adventure, and the adventure has to be well-trimmed, convenient, not too difficult, and virtually risk-free. Canoeists want to drive to wilderness and don't want to have to portage or work too hard to fulfill the quest. And there is the need for signs — for everything because we need to be prompted and told what to do and where to do it. The world of adventure is changing, and our level of preparedness is often deficient, whether we are well-geared or not.

But even with all the changes there is one thing that remains constant, and that's the need to escape the sometimes tedious monotony of life inside the box. The trails we may take and the tribulations along the way that sometimes surface, remind us of our mortality and what we still have to learn about Nature and the wilderness. And when we take the time to explore uncharted paths and learn to live within our expectations, life outside the box becomes more of an enlightening experience and not so much a life and death struggle. You know you've reached that point when you feel less vulnerable while on the wilderness trail than you do when trying to re-assimilate back into the mainstream. The more we climb out of our box and explore the world and ourselves, the less vulnerable we are while on the trail, and the more vulnerable we often become when we try to climb back in.

ABOUT *the* AUTHOR

Ancient Pine by Hap Wilson.

"Protecting our forests... more than just saving trees"

Hap Wilson has travelled over 60,000 kilometres by canoe and snowshoe and embarked on more than three hundred wilderness expeditions. A self-taught writer, artist, and photographer, he is also one of North America's best-known wilderness guides and the author of several books. Wilson recently received the prestigious Bill Mason Award for lifelong achievement in river conservation. He is also co-founder of the environmental group Earthroots and has been building sustainable trails for over thirty years. For more information please visit Hap's website at www.eskakwa.ca.

ABOUT INGRID ZSCHOGNER

(Illustrator)

Wolf Eyes by Ingrid Zschogner.

Ingrid Zschogner is a self-taught artist and outdoor enthusiast and has been creating detailed portraits in oil, graphite, and pastel for over fifteen years. Zschogner is also a professional trailbuilder, wilderness guide, and environmental activist. To view Ingrid's portfolio, visit her website at www.wildrosedesigns.ca.